WINN LIBRARY
Gordon College
Wenham, Mass. 019__    W9-BLN-322

# Language Training in Early Childhood Education

DISCARDED
JENKS LRC
GORDON COLLEGE

# LANGUAGE TRAINING
# IN EARLY
# CHILDHOOD EDUCATION

**Edited by Celia Stendler Lavatelli**

Published for the ERIC Clearinghouse on Early Childhood Education
by the University of Illinois Press

**Third printing, 1974**

© 1971 by The Board of Trustees of the University of Illinois.
Manufactured in the United States of America.
Library of Congress Catalog Card Number 72-141519

**ISBN** 0-252-00116-8

LB
1139
.L3
L33

# Introduction

A noted authority on the subject of language has pointed out that the ability to learn language is so deeply rooted in man that children learn it even in the face of dramatic handicaps. The grammar that they acquire may not be the King's English, but even children from impoverished, disorganized homes know and use all parts of speech by the time they enter kindergarten. Their very mistakes reveal that they have acquired the rules. When a child says "footses" for "feet," he is revealing a knowledge of one of our rules for forming plurals; he is simply not aware of all the exceptions.

In spite of the child's natural capacity for language and his remarkable progress in this area in a few years' time, teachers in Head Start and public school classrooms enrolling disadvantaged children are concerned about language development. They recognize that one of the great handicaps of the disadvantaged lies in the area of meaningful communication. Most of the children from poverty-stricken homes have difficulty in making words do what they want them to do and, in particular, in using language to meet the cognitive demands of the school.

Early childhood curricula typically list, and rightly so, the development of language competence as a goal; language is the vehicle of school instruction and the child who does not have adequate possession of language is handicapped in school learning. That the lower-class child is so handicapped is evidenced by scores on standardized tests of school achievement which show that the lower the socioeconomic class, the greater the number of students who score below grade. The disability is particularly marked in reading; disadvantaged seventh and eighth graders who test at the third-grade level are not uncommon. Such low scores have been attributed to

many factors: little desire to succeed in school, lack of readiness
for school learning, poor teaching, and, most frequently, a language
disability.

What aspect of the lower-class child's language deficit affects
school achievement is still a matter of study. It is generally agreed
that the disadvantaged child has a smaller vocabulary than his
middle-class peer, and that he uses substandard English. But whether
vocabulary size or usage affects school learning is debatable. Not
knowing five synonyms for "beautiful" and saying "he done it" are
unlikely to impede school learning. What is more likely to interfere
(and there is a growing conviction on this point) is the disadvantaged child's inability to use language to meet the demands of the
school. When he is asked to follow directions, participate in discussion, compare two objects or events and make discriminations between them, classify or draw inferences, he is often at a loss to do so.

What kind of training procedures should be followed to overcome
a language deficit is also a matter of study. At the present time several positions with respect to training prevail. One is the "English-as-
a-second-language" approach, a position which assumes that whatever the child has by way of language is too poor to be built upon,
and so English must be taught as if it were a second language. The
remedy according to this school of thought is to program the child's
mind with certain sentence patterns which will enable him to express
ideas. These language patterns are taught to children in a highly repetitive fashion. The Bereiter-Engelmann model is perhaps the best-
known example of the second-language approach. A second position
is represented by nursery school educators who advocate a balance
between a structured and an unstructured program. They believe
that an environment where language production is encouraged in
sociodramatic play and show-and-tell activities is highly conducive
to language development. In addition, they hold that short periods of
instruction devoted to sorting activities, games involving description
of objects, and the like will provide needed remedial training. A third
approach is that in which the natural method of language learning
is systematized. Those who advocate the natural method argue that
the normal child has a biological capacity for language of which he
can avail himself if the environment provides stimulation and opportunity. An impoverished environment may result in a deficit in lan-

guage production but not in language capacity. The deficit can be overcome in part by sufficient exposure to well-formed English sentences addressed to the child and to which he must make a response. The sentences provide the raw material which the child can process to find relations in sentences and the rules for forming them. To further overcome the deficit, the teacher systematically provides models of the syntactic structures[1] that have been selected to move the child's language practice to a higher level.

The papers in this volume are devoted to both the theory and practice of language training. No attempt has been made to present all points of view. Rather, selection of papers has been made on the basis of what appear to be promising practices in language training derived from current psycholinguistic thought. By the term "psycholinguistic" we refer to contributions of both linguists and developmental psychologists to the study of language acquisition. Linguists have contributed to our knowledge of what constitutes the structure of a language and to an understanding of the relations expressed in verbal behavior. They search for a mathematics that will describe the way in which the speaker of a language understands collections of words and relationships among them. Developmental psychologists, for their part, have contributed to our knowledge of how linguistic processes develop as the child grows up. Consider, for example, the development of the processes of negation as described by Bellugi-Klima. From a stage where the child expresses negation by putting "no" in front of everything, as in the sentences "No bed," "No go toilet," "No got candy," the child gradually progresses to a stage where he may sprinkle negatives throughout the sentence, as in "I don't got no candy." Eventually, given the proper models, he proceeds to the acceptable standard form employing only one negative.

A word should be said here about the meaning of "syntax" and "grammar" as used in this volume. Readers who are new to the

[1] A list of syntactic structures useful for such systematic modeling has been prepared by Ursula Bellugi-Klima and Wilbur Hass for the National Laboratory on Early Childhood Education. The structures, with examples, are listed in order of complexity as judged by the age at which they appear in child language. The list, entitled "Syntactical Structures for Modeling in Preschool Language Training," may be ordered from ERIC/ECE Clearinghouse, 805 West Pennsylvania, Urbana, Illinois, at a cost of 35 cents.

field of psycholinguistics may associate such words with the study of correct usage as they knew it in school. In fact, some readers may be raising a question about why preschool teachers bother with such things as syntax and grammar. However, the terms as used today are not as narrowly defined as they were a generation ago. Today the term "syntax" is used to refer to the way in which words are put together in a sentence to convey meaning. As for the term "grammar," as used by the linguist, the word does not refer to use of standard English (in our language) but to the patterns by which units called morphemes are built into words ("box" plus "-es" to make "boxes," for example), and the words built into phrases (noun or verb phrases).

Part I is devoted to some theoretical issues. The first paper, by Donald Moore, is a critical examination of current thought and practice in language training. Readers will find it valuable as a thorough and thoughtful survey of the literature and as a clear statement of the language difficulties of the disadvantaged. The paper by Hass presents an analysis of competence in what psycholinguists call "deep" structures. "Deep" structures are used in contrast to surface structures. To teach a child to say "This is a cup" is to teach him a surface structure. To teach a child language in such a way that he can describe what he has in mind by a cup so that another person knows what is in his mind is teaching him to deal with deep structures. As Dr. Hass points out, the latter procedure is training the child in the full potentiality of natural language. The Sigel paper examines a particular aspect of language; namely, the ability to use language to talk about objects or events that are distant in time or space from the object or event itself. As the reader will be reminded often in this volume, the lack of ability to use language to talk about things which are not in the immediate present has often been described as a deficit in lower-class language.

Part II deals with training procedures. Dr. Painter's paper describes a successful program in infant training that has been tried out at the University of Illinois. Many specialists have been advocating the provision of a stimulating environment during the infancy period as essential to proper development. Some would argue that it is particularly important to provide stimulation during the critical period of primary-language acquisition and that the period beginning before the first birthday and extending through the preschool years constitutes this critical period. Middle-class mothers appear to be natural teachers in this respect. That is, they talk to babies, play games with them, and engage them in activities demanding language without ever being instructed to do so. Many lower-class mothers have never seen other mothers interacting with babies in this fashion and thus do not systematically provide infants with the verbal environment conducive to language development. Dr. Painter's paper is sufficiently detailed to be helpful to the reader wishing to initiate an infant-training program for lower-class mothers. "A Systematized Approach to the Tucson Method of Language Teaching" describes a model of language teaching developed by Marie Hughes and her staff at the University of Arizona, Tucson, for disadvantaged Mexican-American children. The model used the systematized approach to the natural method described on page vi. As teachers carry on stimulating activities with the children, they use models of well-formed sentences including syntactic structures at a level higher than the child is using. In this way, they provide a "language lift" for the child. Finally, in Part II comes Courtney Cazden's very interesting report on language programs in British infant schools, schools which are being studied avidly by American educators at the present time. Not only does Dr. Cazden give us a vivid account of language learning in the British schools, but she also makes some practical and penetrating suggestions for application of what she has seen.

Although Part III is entitled "Evaluation," no attempt has been made to review all of the evaluation procedures in vogue today. Dr. Bellugi-Klima's paper describes a language comprehension test which teachers will find useful.

As teachers work with children to improve their use of language, they want to know how well the children are doing. Exactly how much an individual child knows about language is not always clear from what he says. He may know how to put sentences together in particular ways, but we may not happen to hear him using certain constructions.

One goal in language programs is to raise the level of sophistication of the child's expression. Suppose a child only uses the present tense in his speech, even when he talks about events in the past.

Suppose he says, for example, "We go store and buy candy," even when he is talking about something that has already happened. We want to raise his language level by having him use the past tense, "We *went* to the store and *bought* candy." (We want to do this, by the way, not because it is more genteel or middle class to speak standard English, but because use of the past tense helps both speaker and listener to place an event in time, and so is an aid to clear communication. Not all rules of standard English are essential to clear communication, but many of them are.) The question is, does the child know how to talk about past events and simply not use the past tense? Or is it the case that the child simply does not know how to change the tense of the verb to denote a past event? In the first case, the child's competence is not an issue, but only his performance. In the second case, both competence and performance are inadequate. The paper by Dr. Bellugi-Klima contains some evaluation measures which teachers can use to find out whether or not a child has a particular grammatical form even though the teacher may not hear him use it.

The Slobin and Welsh paper examines the use of imitation as a tool in studying language development. There is considerable agreement among linguists that children do not acquire language through imitation. In fact, one of the interesting points brought out in this paper is that the child will not repeat a sentence using grammatical rules that are not a part of his own repertoire. That is, children can repeat correctly only that which is formed by rules they have already mastered. Again, the procedures described by Slobin and Welsh can be used by preschool teachers to evaluate informally the language development of individual children.

It is hoped that this volume of papers will make readers much more conscious of language processes and of the components of teacher-child interactions that affect language acquisition. Hopefully, too, teacher-readers will grow in appreciation of what a fascinating area the study of language acquisition is and will be able to apply in the classroom some of the findings from psycholinguistic theory presented here.

Celia Stendler Lavatelli
Urbana, Illinois
June, 1969

# Contents

# Contributors

Dr. Ursula Bellugi-Klima
The Salk Institute for Biological
  Studies
San Diego, California

Dr. Courtney Cazden
Graduate School of Education
Harvard University
Cambridge, Massachusetts

Dr. Wilbur Hass
Shimer College
Mt. Carroll, Illinois

Dr. Donald Moore
University of Illinois
Chicago, Illinois

Dr. Genevieve Painter
Family Education Association of
  Champaign
Champaign, Illinois

Dr. Irving Sigel
Department of Psychology
State University of New York
Buffalo, New York

Dr. Daniel Slobin
Department of Psychology
University of California
Berkeley, California

Mr. Charles Welsh
University of California
Berkeley, California

*Editor*
Dr. Celia Stendler Lavatelli
College of Education
University of Illinois
Urbana, Illinois

# PART I

## Some Theoretical Considerations

# 1

DONALD R. MOORE

# Language Research and Preschool Language Training

## Introduction

Much recent attention has been focused on the possibility of intervening at an early age in the lives of so-called "disadvantaged" children to attenuate alleged deficiencies in their language development which limit later educability. This paper is a selective and critical review of theory and empirical investigations relevant to specifying the nature of such a program. It draws primarily on work in linguistics, psycholinguistics, and sociolinguistics which illuminates the patterns of language development in children and the nature of American subcultural differences in language development.

This analysis is seen as one part of a program of analysis and research necessary to specify the answers to two related questions:

1. What specific subcultural differences in language ability limit the educability of "disadvantaged" preschool children?
2. What instructional methods and situations will be most effective in teaching these abilities?

The bulk of this paper is devoted to the first question. Much less evidence exists on the second question, and the conclusions of the section on instructional methods must be regarded as especially tentative. The aim of both major parts, however, is not to provide definitive answers that can be immediately translated into widespread programs, but rather to provide specifically stated hypotheses that can be tested in training experiments.

## I. Locating the "Disadvantaged"

The terms "lower class," "disadvantaged," and "subcultural differences" are used in this paper. With reference to the use of these terms, it is important to make two points clear:

1. Only a small subset of the total set of language differences observed between individuals and between groups puts certain individuals or groups at an educational disadvantage.
2. Group designations (such as social class) should be regarded only as gross preliminary classifications that are useful at this stage in research on language and education. They should not be employed to prescribe identical language programs for every individual who falls into a given social group.

With respect to the first point, the study of subcultural language differences and the development of language programs have been plagued with the unquestioned assumption that any deviation from the standards of white middle-class speech puts the "deviant" child at a disadvantage and must be remedied (see page 11). An important theme running through this paper is the attempt to distinguish among the many observed subcultural differences in language use in order to isolate those differences which have the most important consequences for educability and should thus be the focus of a preschool language program.

With respect to the second point, it is crucial that the reader understand the sense in which racial and social class designations are employed in this paper and the relation that they should have to the design of educational programs.

This paper reviews many studies that have employed a child's "social class" and "race" as independent variables and that have employed as dependent variables various aspects of the child's language use. The use of social class as an independent variable in the study of linguistic development raises particularly difficult problems, because as Lesser, Fifer, and Clark point out: "Although the assessment and interpretation of social class characteristics has been studied for many years, no generally adopted concept for the measurement of membership in a social class has emerged. Membership has been variously viewed as a way of life, the exercise of power over persons and resources, or a composite of objective properties such as occupation, education and area of dwelling" (Lesser, Fifer, and Clark, 1965, p. 25).

What is the relevance of these sociological investigations for the development of educational programs for preschool children? A moderately large correlation has been consistently observed between social class (as measured by simple objective indicators like occupation of family head) and measures associated with school success. For example, intelligence and academic achievement both correlate about .4 with social class (Bloom, Davis, and Hess, 1965, pp. 98, 177).

Thus, it seems a reasonable strategy in developing information about the nature of the abilities children bring to the educational process to investigate differences between various social class groups. It seems a useful working hypothesis to say that families occupying a similar position on social class indicator scales might more often than not have certain attitudes and objective circumstances in common which would influence (and sometimes limit) their children's development in ways that have important consequences for their educability.

It should be apparent, however, that if one finds a correlation of .4 between social class and intelligence, for example, this does not indicate that all lower-class children possess a certain type of disability and should thus be given the same type of educational treatment. This is clearly indicated by the results of a study of the IQ's of grade school children in Riverside, California (Wilson, 1967, p. 173). The mean IQ of white lower-class boys was 98, while the mean for boys from professional families was 111. Nevertheless, about a quarter of the lower-class children ranked above the mean for the professional children. Clearly, it is ludicrous to assume that all lower-class children in Riverside are "disadvantaged" and should receive the same type of compensatory educational program, even though the average lower-class child is 13 points below the average professional child in tested IQ.

Thus, the terms "lower-class child" and "middle-class child," as they are employed in the rest of this paper, should be considered only to apply to the average child within a given group in a given study and not to any individual child (unless his particular characteristics are compared to group norms). The same qualification applies to the use of racial designations and to the term "subculture," which is used as a handy shorthand term for a combination of race and social class.

With these qualifications in mind, one can examine some of the basic work in linguistics that has contributed to the study of subcultural language differences.

## II.  Relevant Distinctions from Transformational Grammar

Several important facts about the nature of language, explicated by Chomsky (1957), force on us a notion of language quite different from that formulated, for example, by traditional learning theory. First, language is rule-bound and the nature of these rules is much more complex than the traditional notion of "association." Second, the system of rules that a speaker employs enables him to speak and understand an indefinitely large number of sentences which are novel to him but which are a consistent extension of his rule system. It is, in Chomsky's view, the fundamental task of linguistics to provide a formal characterization of the nature of these rules. An idealized version of the speaker-listener's language, which Chomsky calls his language "competence," is distinct from "performance" or the actual use of language: "We thus make a fundamental distinction between competence (the speaker-hearer's knowledge of his language) and performance (the actual use of language in concrete situations)" (Chomsky, 1965, p. 4).

Chomsky and those who have followed his transformational grammar approach have attempted to develop rules of language competence for what have generally been considered the three main areas of language study: syntax, phonology, and semantics. The approach has proved most effective in the study of phonology (sound patterns) and syntax (roughly, relations between words in sentences) (Klima, 1964a; Halle, 1964; Chomsky, 1965; Rosenbaum, 1965). Although some attempts have been made to apply the transformational approach to semantics or language meaning (Katz and Postal, 1964), this area of study is not nearly as well developed as the study of syntax and phonology.

The first part of this paper is broadly organized around the three major areas which have been of concern to students of language as they apply to the development of a preschool language curriculum. Section III deals with studies of syntactic and phonological competence. Section IV deals with performance factors, primarily as they influence patterns of language syntax. Section V deals with studies of semantics.

A final introductory point requires clarification with respect to linguistic theory. The types of grammars that the linguist writes are not intended as models of the actual psychological processes by which people produce and comprehend sentences (i.e., in the sense that the order of rules in a grammar has some relationship to the temporal order of processes of a person understanding sentences or that the complexity of the grammatical description of a sentence is related to the difficulty a listener might have in understanding it) (Chomsky, 1965, p. 9). It may be that some such relations exist, but this is a hypothesis that requires testing in each individual situation.

## III. Subcultural Differences in Syntax and Phonology

The use of grammatical analysis by Chomsky's methods has proved extremely valuable in the empirical study of the development of children's language and in the analysis of subcultural differences in children's language. Basic work on language acquisition has been done by Brown, Cazden, and Bellugi-Klima (1971), who have collected longitudinal data on the mother-child language interactions of three children (Adam, Eve, and Sarah). Their analysis has demonstrated that from the earliest two-word utterances, children's language can be described by the types of syntactic rules Chomsky has outlined (Brown and Bellugi, 1964) and that later developments in the syntax of these children can also be described effectively using the rules of transformational grammar (Bellugi, 1966, 1967).

The success of the transformational approach with these subjects has suggested to a number of investigators that it might be an extremely useful way of describing subcultural language differences. The fact that the language of Brown's subjects was found to follow rules at each stage of its development suggests that the language of lower-class Negro and white children must be viewed much differently that it has been by many past investigators (Templin, 1957; Pederson, 1964; Williamson, 1965). These investigators have assumed that any deviation from the idealized standard English of the high school grammar book is an unsystematic "error" on the part of the speaker. Thus, Templin notes that lower-class white children say "I got" and "I can" instead of "I have" and "I may" (Templin, 1957, p. 96); Pederson finds that Negro children say "fo" instead of "for" (Pederson, 1964, p. 33); and Williamson, that Negroes tend to say "dentis" instead of "dentist" (Williamson, 1965, p. 25).

Just as the work of the Brown group has established that the speech of the child is not a random deviation from adult norms, so analysis of the speech of various subcultural groups has demonstrated that it too is in conformity with a rule system of its own. For example, Klima (1964b) has described the syntactic rules that differentiate four dialects in their use of "who" and "whom" in relative clauses. Labov and Cohen (1966, p. 11) describe the rules that generate "I asked Alvin if he knows how to play basketball" in standard dialect, but "I asked Alvin do he know how to play basketball" in certain Negro dialects. Labov (1968) has also analyzed phonological rules underlying Negro dialects in New York.

The fact that rules of phonological and syntactic competence underlie the language of children from diverse subcultural groups provides a useful framework in which to evaluate three hypotheses about language differences among subcultural groups which have implications for the development of a compensatory language curriculum:

1.  Phonological and syntactic differences between speakers of American dialects cause difficulties in mutual intelligibility.
2.  Speakers of certain dialects have fewer syntactic rules in their grammar and thus their dialect is a less adequate device for communicating ideas.
3.  There are not major differences in the grammatical rules employed by various subcultural groups, but certain groups are slower in their rate of development of these rules (based on Cazden, 1967a).

## A. Differences in Language and Differences in Intelligibility

Two types of evidence can be brought to bear on the analysis of phonological and syntactic differences and their consequences for intelligibility between speakers. First, the extent of divergence between the phonological and syntactic rule systems for various dialects can *suggest* the nature of possible difficulties in intelligibility between speakers. The primary focus of this discussion will be on differences between rule systems of Negro dialects and standard English, since Negro dialects generally constitute more extreme divergences from standard English than the speech of lower-class whites. (Loban, 1966, shows this clearly in spite of the fact that he treats deviations from standard English only as "errors.")

It should be noted that many Negroes do not speak a distinct dialect; the largest differences occur in the case of southern rural Negroes. As Negroes live in the north they tend to adopt more and more features of the standard dialect (Labov, 1967, p. 143). Nevertheless, the work of several investigators reveals syntactic and phonological differences between the dialects of some Negro groups and whites. Below is a list of syntactic differences isolated by a number of empirical studies of children's language (Labov and Cohen, 1966; Labov, 1967; Loban, 1966; Baratz, 1968; New York City Board of Education, 1968):

1. Omission of "s" in third person singular ("He walk" instead of "He walks").
2. Use of double negatives and "ain't."
3. Omission of the possessive ("Mary husband" instead of "Mary's husband").
4. Omission of the verb "be" in present tense copulative sentences ("He sick" instead of "He's sick").
5. Nonstandard "if-did" construction ("Ask Alvin do he want to play basketball" instead of "Ask Alvin if he wants to play basketball").
6. Lack of subject-verb agreement ("We is here now." "You is too much").
7. Nonstandard future tense ("I'm a hit you." "He goin' hit you").
8. Omission of "do" in some questions ("How he fix that?").
9. "Be" in place of other "be" forms ("He be in the hallway").
10. Omission of the past tense ("He walk" instead of "He walked").
11. Aspect use of "be" ("He be tired" meaning "He's always tired").

On its face, this list does not suggest that syntactic differences between dialects present major barriers to intelligibility between Negro and white speakers. For example, the first nine differences listed do not involve the loss of important semantic information (e.g., the possessive relationship is still clear from word position even with the "s" omitted; "be" in present tense copulative sentences carries no semantic information and is omitted in some languages).

Additional careful study of these syntactic differences further undercuts their importance within the grammatical system. Labov finds that the "-ed" is often present in the Negro child's speech and accounts for its lack in many sentences on the basis of phonological rather than syntactic rules (specifically the simplification of final consonant clusters) (Labov, 1967, p. 158). He also concludes that the omission of the copulative form only occurs in certain grammatical contexts but is basically present in the child's grammar (Labov and Cohen, 1966, p. 6).

Analysis of speech samples from a group of two-year-old lower-class Boston Negroes failed to find several of the differences cited by other investigators. Cazden (1967b, p. 17) reports that the possessives, past markers, and third person indicatives (and also plurals and progressives) were developing in the same patterns in the grammar of her lower-class Negro subjects as were those of the subjects studied by the Brown group.[1]

Working with the same sample, I compared stages in the development of copulatives in Cazden's subjects with those I observed in Brown's. I found three stages in copulative development, each characterized by a distinct grammatical rule, which were identical both for Brown's subjects and Cazden's lower-class Negro subjects (Moore, 1968, p. 17).

The last difference cited on page 9, the aspect use of "be," seems somewhat more basic in terms of grammatical rules (Stewart, 1965, p. 60). Along with the absence of the past marker, it is also a syntactic difference which could give rise to semantic misunderstand-

[1] Cadzen did not gather background information (parents' occupation and education) on her subjects, but rather based the judgment that they were disadvantaged on the fact that they spent all day in a day care center where they received almost no language stimulation. It would seem a valid inference to consider these children as comparable to the children designated lower-class in other studies, but the reader may question this judgment.

ings between speakers from different subcultural groups. It does not, however, seem to be used by all Negro speakers. It is not present in the protocols of Cazden's Boston Negro subjects.

The most complete phonological analysis of Negro and white children has been done by Labov (1968). Here is a list of the major types of differences he observed, as summarized in Labov (1967):

1. Omission of "r" before consonants or as a final sound (guard = god, court = caught).
2. Omission of "l" before consonants or as a final sound (toll = toe, help = hep).
3. Simplification of consonant clusters at the ends of words (past = pass, rift = riff, meant = men, mend = men, hold = hole, let's = les, that's = thas).
4. Weakening of final consonant (boot = boo).

What are the effects of these phonological differences between white and Negro dialect? As Labov argues, they create a number of homonyms for the Negro speaker that are distinct in the standard dialect (Labov, 1967, p. 113). However, the standard dialect also contains a great many homonyms which appear frequently in everyday speech (e.g., "there" and "their"). Generally, the correct alternative from a pair of homonyms is distinguishable from its context. Thus, the phonological patterns of the Negro dialect somewhat increase a problem that is common in all languages and must be dealt with by all speakers and listeners.

As stated earlier, differences between the syntax and phonology of different groups can only *suggest* differences in actual speech performance, in this case difficulties in intelligibility. Before significance of the syntactic and phonological differences outlined above can be interpreted further, it is necessary to consider some of the evidence on actual language performance.

Recent sociolinguistic research has focused particularly on the nature of communication between persons speaking different dialects or languages. The picture that emerges is that individuals are extremely flexible in comprehending and speaking a variety of languages and dialects. The monolingualism of most American speakers is atypical in the world; the majority of the world's people speak two languages or at least two quite distinct dialects (Macnamara,

1967, p. 2). Such languages or dialects are generally used in distinct realms of activity, and thus speakers use suitable codes in different situations. For example, many countries employ one dialect for formal interactions and another in the home (Ferguson, 1964, p. 429). Or, in a society with a rigid social structure, the type of dialect one uses may be defined by one's social position as it relates to another person (Gumperz, 1964, p. 150). Or it may vary systematically with the topic of conversation (Gumperz, 1964, p. 151). Conversations between speakers of distinct dialects who can understand one another but cannot speak the dialect of the other person are extremely common in many communities (Ervin-Tripp, 1967, p. 82). Even in relatively homogeneous speech communities there are still systematic shifts in style governed by the nature of the social interaction — for example, shifts in method of addressing a person (Ervin-Tripp, 1967, p. 8).

There is a good deal of evidence that this sort of flexibility is also present in speakers from various subcultural groups within the United States. For example, Stewart (1965, p. 58) describes the facility of a group of Negroes in Bloomington, Indiana, in switching from a standard English dialect spoken with outsiders to a private Negro dialect spoken on social occasions within their group.

Of particular interest are several types of investigations of children's abilities to comprehend dialects they do not speak. First, Deutsch (1967, p. 194) administered the Wepman Auditory Discrimination Test to Negro and white first and fifth graders of various social classes. This test requires the child to tell whether pairs of words pronounced in the standard dialect are the same or different. There were no significant Negro-white differences at either grade level. A similar and much more stringent test was made by Labov (1967, p. 160) on some of his Negro subjects. He asked them to discriminate between the present and past tense of several verbs, employing distinctions the boys didn't make in their own speech (e.g., "mess" vs. "messed"). None had any trouble making such distinctions. Thus, on a phonological level, the work of Deutsch and Labov suggests that children from different subcultural groups can readily hear sound distinctions in standard English that they don't make themselves.

Cherry-Piesach (1965) attempted to assess the ability of Negro and white first and fifth graders from various social class backgrounds to understand their teacher and their fellow classmates. Using the Cloze procedure, she systematically deleted words from samples of teacher and pupil speech and asked her subjects to fill appropriate words into these spaces. Of course, this task taps far more than difficulties stemming from differences in dialect, as its significant correlation with IQ suggests. Of six measures of the quality of fill-ins in the teacher's speech sample (three at each grade), only one showed a significant Negro-white difference, and this difference disappeared when IQ was controlled. On the children's speech samples, Negroes and whites performed equally on Negro samples, but whites were superior to Negroes on white samples. If this represents a difficulty caused by differences in phonology or syntax between Negroes and whites, then it is a one-way difference, since white scores were equal to those of Negroes on Negro speech samples.

Investigators who have employed sentence-imitation tasks with Negroes and whites provide further evidence regarding intelligibility between subcultural groups. They (Labov and Cohen, 1966; Osser, 1967; and Baratz, 1968) report that Negro children, asked to imitate sentences in standard English, systematically shift the phonology and syntax of the sentence into their own dialect. Both Osser and Baratz found this to be true with the major syntactic differences between Negro and white grammar outlined in page 9. In addition, Baratz tested white children on imitation of sentences in Negro dialect and found similar shifts toward the white children's own grammar. Let's look closely at an example of this phenomenon to draw out its implications for intelligibility. If a boy is asked to imitate "Ask Alvin if he wants to play basketball," and responds, "Ask Alvin do he want to play basketball," it is clear that he has (a) understood the sentence, and (b) shifted to its semantic and syntactic equivalent in his own language system. Thus, the ability to understand a dialect one doesn't speak is clearly present in the lower-class preschool Negro subjects tested by Osser and Baratz, as well as the adolescents tested by Labov.

Linguistic and psycholinguistic evidence from a variety of situations then seems to have clear implications for a preschool compensatory program. It has been shown that the syntactic and phonological differences among the languages of various American subcultures are relatively minor, that speakers throughout the world have a great flexibility for communicating across dialect barriers and can readily understand dialects they don't speak, and that Negro lower-class preschool children have demonstrated that they can understand phonological and syntactic structures they don't use themselves. Thus, on grounds of mutual intelligibility there seems to be no reason for the educator to attempt to teach the child to speak the standard dialect. The evidence indicates that a child who is exposed to this dialect will be able to understand it without speaking it. The preschool child who speaks a nonstandard dialect should be exposed to a speech model from the standard dialect, perhaps with special emphasis on discriminating distinctions in the standard dialect different from those in the nonstandard dialect.

Some have asserted that the child's speech patterns must be changed for social reasons even if other problems do not exist. For example, Loban (1966, p. 1) argues that nonstandard language patterns stigmatize a child in the essentially white middle-class society with which he must deal. In addition to the moral arguments that might be made against such a position, there are a number of practical ones. First, contact with members of one's family and peer group who use one's own dialect are a powerful counterforce against changes in pronunciation and syntax (Cohen, 1966, p. 74). Attempts to change the dialect of random groups of children have consistently failed (John, 1967, p. 5), including one training attempt that went on for three years (Lin, 1965). It appears that a person must have a specific motivating reason to change his speech habits, and this motivation is not likely to be found in the lower-class preschool child. Constant "correction" of the child's speech is likely to cause only antagonism and frustration and should be avoided in a compensatory preschool program.

## B. Missing Syntactic Rules and Slow Development of Syntactic Rules

There may, of course, be many reasons why a lower-class child does not express himself as adequately as a middle-class child. The final two questions raised earlier ask whether such difficulties can be traced to the fact that the lower-class child has fewer syntactic rules in his grammar or that such rules develop at a slower pace for him. Evidence presented in the previous section of this paper is relevant to answering this question. For example, if it were true that the past tense was missing from certain Negro dialects, one might argue (although this hypothesis would have to be put to an empirical test) that the Negro child couldn't understand or express action in the past. As Labov's analysis shows, however, the past tense is not *missing* from Negro dialects, since irregular past forms which are extremely common in everyday speech are used correctly by Negro speakers and since the regular past ("-ed") is often present in the child's speech but is deleted because of consonant-cluster simplification in some contexts (Labov, 1967, p. 157).

Other evidence already presented suggests that basic grammatical markings and patterns are not missing in the early development of the lower-class child's grammar. Cazden found the use of plurals, past markers, possessives, third person indicatives, and progressives to follow the same patterns in lower-class Negro children as in Brown's three middle-class and lower-middle-class children and to be developing at the same ages.[2] My own study of the development of the copulative in Brown's and Cazden's subjects showed that the lower-class Negroes were acquiring the same rules and developing them at the same pace as Adam, Eve, and Sarah (Moore, 1968, p. 17).

Within Brown's small group of subjects, it is possible to compare middle-class Adam and Eve with lower-middle-class Sarah. Although the speech of Sarah's mother is more restricted in some respects than the speech of Adam's and Eve's mother (Cazden, 1967a, p. 12), Sarah's grammatical development was about the same as Adam's in terms of age (although both lagged behind precocious Eve). In addition to age, mean length of utterance has proved a useful scale on which to assess grammatical development. Thus, one can compare the development of various children's grammars when the average length of the sentences they use is equal. On this scale of development Sarah is more advanced than either Adam or Eve. In my study of copulatives, for example, she was the only child of

[2] See footnote 1.

the three to use the adult rule for copulatives in over 90 percent of her utterances before her mean utterance length had reached five morphemes (Moore, 1968, p. 18). The course of Sarah's grammatical development then provides some further support for the position that lower-class children do not have rules missing from their grammar nor do they lag behind the middle class in the acquisition of these rules in the early period of grammatical development.

It might be argued that all children acquire certain basic grammatical structures at a young age but that there are subcultural language differences in the acquisition of more complicated structures acquired at a later age. Bellugi compares lower-middle-class Sarah and middle-class Adam in later grammatical development of rules for negation. She finds no differences between the two on such complicated negative patterns as negation within relative clauses ("That means you don't like it?") and negative tag questions ("This is Boston, isn't it?") (Bellugi, 1967, pp. 127-55).

The best evidence concerning the development of syntactic rules would come from an investigation which collects a large sample of children's speech (Brown, Cazden, and Bellugi-Klima, 1971). Other methods have been employed for testing syntactic development, including sentence imitation, ability to make appropriate transformations of sentences ("Ask the puppet why he's not tired"), ability to decide which of a set of pictures is described by a given sentence, and ability to follow directions which involve various syntactic structures (Cazden, 1967a, p. 148; Bellugi-Klima, 1968; Chomsky, 1968).

Such short-term tests, however, run the danger of underestimating the nature of the child's grammar, since he may be inhibited by the presence of a strange tester, suffer short-term lapses of attention, or be responding to other situational factors that mask his underlying competence. Of course systematic differences in ability in such testing situations are of interest in their own right, but one must be cautious in interpreting them as reflecting differences in grammatical competence.

These investigators have applied such tests to children of different social classes in the later stages of grammatical development (ages four to six). Shriner and Miner (1967) tested the ability of four-year-old children from middle- and lower-class backgrounds to employ appropriate morphological endings (pluralizations, verb endings, and possessives), using a test developed by Berko (1958). The authors do not identify the race of the two social class groups. They found no differences in the mastery of these forms between social classes.

LaCivita, Kean, and Yamamoto (1966) conducted a study (summarized in Cazden, 1970b, p. 2) in which lower-middle- and upper-class elementary school children were asked to give the meaning of nonsense words in sentences such as the following: "Ungubily the mittler *gimmled*" (grammatical signal "-ed" only cue). "A twener *baikels* meedily" (grammatical signal plus position cue). They hypothesized that lower-middle-class children would be less able to give a word that was the same part of speech as the underlined nonsense word. This hypothesis was not confirmed.

Imitation and comprehension of more complex syntactic structures were employed by Osser, Wang, and Zaid. (1969) in comparing five-year-old lower-class Negro and middle-class white children. Both the imitation and comprehension tasks are based on the same 13 grammatical structures. Osser found that the lower-class Negro children made significantly more errors on the comprehension task. He also found that they made significantly more errors on the key grammatical structures on the imitation task, even when the responses on this task were corrected for dialect differences. Osser concludes that his results "strongly suggest that the Negro lower-class group's control over some common syntactic structures in standard English is markedly inferior to that of whites" (p. 1073). This conclusion seems unjustified in the light of a closer examination of the data presented. The average Negro lower-class student got 20 of 26 items correct on the comprehension task (as opposed to 24.3 of 26 for the white middle-class child, and 21.4 of 26 items correct on the imitation task corrected for dialect (as opposed to 23.9 of 26 for the middle-class child). These results are statistically significant, but hardly seem to warrant the conclusion that the control of grammatical structures is "markedly inferior" for the lower-class black child. The relatively small differences observed might be traced to the unfamiliarity of the lower-class Negro child to test situations. In any case, it is clear that the Negro lower-class children exhibited substantial grammatical control of the structures (about 75 percent correct on each test).

A quite different pattern of response has been observed in developmental studies where the lack of a grammatical rule has been inferred. For example, Carol Chomsky (1968) found that until children ages six to ten could use certain prerequisite syntactic forms, they are *never* able to give appropriate responses to instruction that involve some fine points of grammar (e.g., when told to "ask Joe what to feed the doll," such children invariably respond with an answer, "the cucumber," instead of an appropriate question).

As the reader can see, the work that has been done so far in comparing the syntactic development of children across social classes is very fragmentary. Ideally what is needed is a longitudinal study similar to the one conducted by Brown, Cazden, and Bellugi-Klima of the syntactic development of children from different ethnic groups and social class backgrounds.

However, the studies which exist indicate that there are not basic syntactic rules "missing" from the grammars of lower-class white and Negro children, nor is there a lag in the grammatical development of such syntactic rules between subcultural groups. Thus, the development of a child's grammatical competence does not appear to be an important focus for a compensatory language program. As Osser's work suggests, it is not the absence of the grammatical rule in the child's competence that limits his educability, but rather his inability to *use* such rules as efficiently as the middle-class child in particular situations. It is such situational performance differences between subcultural groups that will be considered next.

## IV. The Influence of Situations on Language Performance

Turning from questions of differences in competence to differences in performance, an area of possible subcultural differences in language development is suggested by the emphasis of sociolinguists like Hymes (1964a, 1964b, 1966, 1967) on the interaction of characteristics of the speaker with characteristics of the situation in actual language performance. A child may possess a certain syntactic structure as evidenced by its presence at several places in a large sample of his speech but may not be able to use it in a specific situation. Or he may possess a basic rule (e.g., for the formation of a basic noun-adjective combination) but be unable to apply the rule recursively when the situation demands a greatly elaborated set of adjectives to specify a particular object accurately. A good deal of evidence is accumulating which suggests that important relations exist between the language performance of the individual and the situations in which he performs.

For example, an early study by Young (1941, p. 77) showed significant differences in mean sentence length in four different settings in which children's speech samples were collected. With respect to phonology, Labov (1965, p. 81) found marked variations in situations he called "casual," "careful," "oral reading," and "word list reading." And Cazden summarizes results from the study of two six-year-olds in seven situations where mean sentence length was measured by stating that "the situational variance for each child is greater than the overall differences between the two children" (Cazden, 1967a, p. 148).

Brown, Cazden, and Bellugi-Klima (1971, p. 56), drawing on their longitudinal study, conclude: "There seems to be something like a standard frequency profile for mother to child English . . . and in this profile great inequalities exist even among very simple and familiar constructions." Slobin (1968) presents results from the study of Oakland Negro families that show a similar mother-child frequency profile and further show that there is a markedly different frequency profile when the same mother talks with an adult friend.

With the knowledge that variations in situations are related to variations in language use, several sociolinguists have recently called for the analysis of social setting and social function as an integral part of language analysis: "The rules of verbal output and comprehension must be organized to specify social features" (Ervin-Tripp, 1967, p. 3). Likewise, Hymes (1964b, p. 8) advocates "approaching language and communication in integral relation to social context and function." The goal of this approach is the systematic specification of the ways in which social situations interact with characteristics of speakers to determine language performance. To this end, Ervin-Tripp (1967, p. 53) and Hymes (1964b, p. 15) have developed roughly similar typologies for an integrated description of linguistic and social variables as they affect language performance.

Based on this work, it is useful for the purposes of this paper to distinguish two broad types of situational influences on language performance, which I will characterize as the "social" and "cognitive" demands of the situation. Social demands include such variables as the status and roles of conversants, their attitudes toward language communication, their motives in a particular speech interaction, etc. Cognitive demands include such factors as the complexity of speech required to communicate a given message, the extent to which one can rely on "props" within the situation to ease the burden of communication, the difficulty of the vocabulary required for communicating a given message, etc.

With respect to social class differences in language performance and the cognitive and social demands of situations, challenging hypotheses have been formulated by Bernstein (1962a, 1962b, 1964, 1965, 1967). Central to Bernstein's approach is the contention that most middle-class speakers can employ both a "restricted" and "elaborated" language code, while the lower-class speaker tends to be limited to a "restricted" language code (Bernstein, 1964). One major distinction between the restricted and elaborated codes is that the restricted code is bound closely to a particular situation, while the elaborated code (through the use of specific adjectives, clauses, verb phrases) communicates independent of the specific context (Bernstein, 1965).

Bernstein sees a social class difference in the ability to use the "elaborated" code developing because the lower-class child lives in a closely knit social world where most people he communicates with have a great deal of previously shared information, reducing the need for verbal specificity; where information is often communicated by voice tone and gesture rather than by explicitly verbal means; and where the number of situations that serve as occasions for verbal interaction are limited (Bernstein, 1965).

## A. Cognitive Demands of Communication Situations

In terms of Bernstein's analysis of elaborated and restricted codes, it seems reasonable that the following set of cognitive demands would require an elaborated code:

1. Speakers cannot rely on previously accumulated shared information.
2. The speaker is required to take his listener into account by specifically naming referents which are not present or about which his listener lacks information.
3. The bulk of the communication load falls on the language code itself, as opposed to such extra-linguistic activities as pointing, voice intonation, etc.

It is interesting to note that social class differences in language performance have emerged in such situations. Bernstein compared speech samples of adolescent boys from different social classes in group discussions of capital punishment and found that middle-class speakers used more passives, more complex verbs, and a greater proportion of subordinate clauses (1962b, pp. 225-31).

In a replication of this study, Lawton found that middle-class children used significantly more passives, subordinate clauses in general, adjective clauses, and complex verbs (1964, pp. 185-93). Loban interviewed children each year from first through sixth grade. In these interviews, which dealt partially with past experiences, Loban found that middle-class children used phrases and clauses that were structurally more complex, and that they used more infinitives and more complex noun phrases as subjects of sentences (1963, pp. 46-49).

Krauss and Rotter (1968) have employed an experimental situation in which social class differences consistent with the work of Bernstein, Lawton, and Loban have been observed. In a communication task in which two subjects are separated by a screen, one is asked to communicate to the other the order in which blocks inscribed with nonsense forms should be put on a peg. The key problem then is to describe forms which have no simple labels. Notice that the task makes all the cognitive demands outlined above for situations in which an elaborated code is necessary. With respect to social class, six-year-old lower-class speakers do poorest on the task as senders and receivers, even when they are listening to members of their own social class. Heider (1968) has completed further work on the nature of language used in this situation. Lower-class children use metaphorical descriptions to communicate information ("It's like a boat"). In contrast, the more successful middle-class children use an analytic style, describing specific details of the stimulus ("It has a little opening at the top and there are sharp points on both sides").

Two studies recently completed in England provide further specific information as to the sense in which lower-class preschool children employ a restricted language code.

In a study of the quality of language employed by infant school children in England, P. R. Hawkins collected speech samples in structured situations described as "narrative," "descriptive," and "instructive" (the child was asked in the "instructive" situation to describe the workings of a mechanical toy elephant to a blindfolded experimenter). He found that middle-class children employed nouns more than pronouns in these situations. He also found that middle-class children used a greater number of pronouns which had specific noun referents preceding them (e.g., "They kicked the ball and *it* broke the window"). Hawkins's interpretation of these results bears close similarities to the argument about social class differences in referents that has been developed in this paper.

This difference is important for two reasons: firstly, because it enables the middle class child to elaborate — he can talk about "three big boys" but he cannot talk about "three big they"; and secondly, and more important, the middle class child can be understood outside the immediate context, without reference to the "here and now." His speech can be interpreted on its own, without the pictures if necessary, and he makes no assumption that the listener can see the pictures in front of him and know implicitly who is meant by he, she, it, they. The working class child, on the other hand, does make these assumptions, and his speech is therefore tied to the context in which it occurs (Hawkins, 1969).

The findings of Hawkins with respect to differences in the use of pronouns between social class groups is replicated by Tough (1969) in a study of three-year-olds from middle- and lower-class backgrounds. In addition to being separated by class, Tough's lower-class children are from linguistically poor home environments and her middle-class children are from linguistically rich environments. Interestingly, the groups are matched on IQ scores. In a speech sample collected while the child was playing and engaging in conversation with peers, Tough observed differences in pronoun use (similar to those found by Hawkins), in noun phrase complexity, in verb phrase complexity, in mean sentence length, and in use of subordinate clauses. She also rated sentences according to the extent that they were dependent on the situational context for their meaning and found that the middle-class children used more context-independent sentences.

Several studies which provide information on social class differences in adult speech show findings that are consistent with those of the above studies with children and adolescents. Among the speech differences observed by Schatzman and Strauss when they interviewed adults of different social classes after a natural disaster was the vague specification of people, places, objects, and events by the lower-class respondents. For example, lower-class respondents referred to "them," "some people," "over there," "down by the creek," with no sensitivity to the fact that these descriptions conveyed nothing to a person not familiar with the area or actually present at the time when the events occurred (1955, p. 330). Hess and Shipman collected the speech of mothers from different social classes as they instructed their children in the rules of complicated and unfamiliar games. They found that lower-class mothers were inferior to middle-class mothers on several indices of grammatical complexity and that the quality of the mother's speech correlated with performance on the tasks (1965, p. 875).

Also consistent with Bernstein's hypothesis are the results of several investigations in which differences in language complexity failed to appear. Deutsch et al. (1967, p. 196) collected language samples from first and fifth graders using a brightly flashing clown with a tape recorder inside, who urged the children to talk. In the resulting speech samples of what Deutsch calls "spontaneous speech," there were no social class differences in subordination, the only measure of speech complexity employed. Thus, this situation, free from the types of cognitive demands cited on page 21 failed to elicit social class differences in sentence elaboration.

In my own work on the copulative development of children, I examined the complexity of the subjects of copulative sentences in the speech protocols collected for Brown's middle-class and Cazden's lower-class children. In the mother-child interactions of the Brown protocols, over 90 percent of the subjects of copulative sentences used by both mothers and children were pronouns (like "that's," "it's," "there's," "here's," "he's") and less than ten percent were specific nouns or noun phrases. In a situation where most objects or persons discussed are perceptually present and where there is a great deal of shared information between speakers, there is little need for the precise specification of the subjects of utterances. In other words, the cognitive demands for use of an elaborated code were not present, and with respect to the precision with which the subjects of utterances were specified a restricted code was employed by both mothers and children. Comparable results were found with the lower-class children in Cazden's speech samples, which were collected while the children discussed pictures in books.

One might hypothesize that in situations which impose the cognitive demands listed on page 21, the middle-class children should demonstrate a differential ability to specify the subjects of their utterances precisely, using more complex noun phrases as sentence subjects. Some support for this speculation comes from a study of French children by Bresson (cited in Ervin-Tripp and Slobin, 1966, p. 451). He found that children tended to use vague referents for objects unless they were not perceptually present, although the names of the objects were quite familiar to them.

An interesting example of the use of a restricted code with respect to specificity of reference is contained in the protocol of one of Cazden's lower-class subjects, Gerald. Gerald is the most advanced child in grammatical development in Cazden's sample on the basis of his cumulative score on her five measures of grammatical development (Cazden, 1965, p. 79). His mean length of utterance at the beginning of her experiment is 5.20 morphemes, which is greater than any of the middle-class children studied by Brown at comparable ages. Yet for all of his grammatical sophistication, Gerald employs a striking vagueness of reference. Here are some sentences from the beginning of the first sample of his speech collected by Cazden:

> And dere some more right dere.
> Dere a other girl right here.
> And dere some more right here.
> You can put dem in here.
> I gon' put dis one in 'nere.
> I already have some — in nere.
> Den gon' put dis one back in here cause it fell out

Gerald's language use illustrates well two major points made in this paper thus far. The grammatical competence of the lower-class child is not inferior on the average to that of the middle-class child; it is in aspects of his language performance that one finds important social class differences.

In summary, there is a large and growing body of evidence that the cognitive demands listed on page 21 are met inadequately by the lower-class child in language communication. Furthermore, the social class language differences that have appeared when such demands have been placed on the child should serve as an important focus for a compensatory language program. Specifically, one focus of a compensatory language program should be to develop the ability of lower-class children to use language which employs an elaborated syntax that includes the use of subordinates, complex noun phrases, complex verbs, passives, and modification by infinitives and phrases. Particularly important is a precise language of reference which enables the child to specify the characteristics of objects precisely and accurately enough so that the description is not dependent on visual "props" in the situation.

## B. Social Demands of Communication Situations

The second broad category of situational influences in language performance was called "social demands." In this area, also, Bernstein's hypotheses and empirical investigations provide an important insight into social class differences that should be taken into account in a preschool compensatory language program. Bernstein argues that in her verbal communications with her child the lower-class mother tends to be "status" rather than "person" oriented. Thus, she is likely to regard her child's requests for information (especially if they are pressed) as a challenge to her status. The middle-class mother, in contrast, is more oriented to the personal development of her child's intellect; thus she sees a child's questions not as challenges to her status but as requests for information that will further his individual development (Bernstein, 1967, p. 92). The effect of negative reactions to the child's verbal questions will not only retard his intellectual development ("shut up!" is less informative than "the glass is made of plastic so it won't break") but will also depress the child's general use of language.

Some empirical support exists for this line of argument. Hess and Shipman (1965, p. 873) asked mothers from different social classes to teach their children how to perform several complicated tasks. Lower-class mothers used more imperatives in this situation and fewer informative instructions.

Other empirical investigations on the instructions that lower- and middle-class mothers give their children as they enter school reveal additional negative attitudes that lower-class children may bring to linguistic interactions in school. By interviewing mothers, Hess and Shipman (1965, p. 877) found that in preparing their children to go to school, middle-class mothers were more likely to encourage their children to learn as much as possible and to ask the teacher questions whenever things were unclear, while lower-class mothers were more likely to tell their children to be obedient and stay out of trouble.

Thus, this fragmentary evidence suggests that the lower-class child enters school with a hesitancy to question, to initiate verbal interactions with adults, and, in general, to gain information through verbal means. This is an important social constraint on language performance that should be dealt with in a compensatory language program.

## V. Studies of Semantics and Cognitive Development

Section III of this paper dealt with hypotheses about social class language differences in the areas of phonology and syntax. The fourth section, on variations in language performance related to communication situations, also dealt with hypotheses about syntax; i.e., syntactic complexity as a variable dependent upon the interaction of characteristics of speakers with characteristics of situations. In addition, the fourth section touched on related issues usually considered to lie in the area of semantics (i.e., the use of precise referential language). Section V discussed additional aspects of semantics which have implications for a compensatory language program.

As was indicated earlier, transformational grammar has not formulated a useful semantic theory. Nor has anyone else. In contrast to the reasonably well-developed areas of phonology and syntax, semantics is a cloudy area where the best empirical information relevant to this paper comes from looking at several very specific areas of study. Some of this work lies on the borderline between studies of language and studies of cognition. Thus, it is sometimes necessary to clarify the language-cognition issues in a given area of research to point out the relevance of that research for the formulation of a compensatory language program.

## A. Vocabulary Studies

Although there are many studies of vocabulary on record, most of them have been conducted within a testing tradition that tells us little about the process by which words and their meanings are acquired and used. Although it is well known that lower-class white and minority-group students generally do worse on such tests than middle-class whites (see, for example, Coleman et al., 1966, pp. 221-51), the fact that these tests focus on the general meanings of uncommon words makes it difficult to interpret such subcultural differences.

A number of distinctions are helpful in interpreting subcultural differences in vocabulary development. First, one should make the distinction common to other areas of language study between comprehension and production. Most studies of vocabulary have concentrated on word comprehension rather than actual word use.

Within the comprehension area, one should distinguish between words which describe objects and activities likely to appear in the child's environment and those which do not. If a lower-class child doesn't know the meaning of "sonata," it is likely to be because he has never been exposed to the word. If he doesn't know the meaning of the word "fireman," however, this may indicate a much more serious type of deficit. Perhaps the lower-class child is less likely to have events and objects coded for him in language, and this results in later difficulties in the process of attaching words to their referents. Of particular interest in this connection are two studies of the comprehension vocabulary of lower-class children. John and Goldstein (1963, p. 268) found that six-year-old lower-class children were inferior to middle-class children in defining words describing common actions, such as "digging." Lesser, Fifer, and Clark (1965, p. 13) found receptive vocabulary differences for first-grade children from different social classes and ethnic groups on a word-meaning test which employed only referents prominent in their urban environment.

Tests of production are rarer than tests of comprehension, but existing studies are consistent in the pattern of their results. Several investigators who have employed the type-token ratio in analyzing speech samples from children of different social classes have found that the lower-class children used fewer different words than middle-class children (e.g., Deutsch, 1967, p. 199). Other investigators have compared the variety of words in specific grammatical categories employed by speakers from different social classes. Bernstein (1962a, p. 299) found that lower-class speakers used fewer uncommon adjectives, adverbs, and conjunctions, and Lawton (1964, p. 193) also found uncommon adjectives and adverbs (as judged by word-frequency counts) less common in lower-class speech. Notice that these findings support Bernstein's contention that lower-class speech should not only be more constrained on the structural syntactic level, but also on the lexical level.

These studies of vocabulary comprehension and production have important implications for a compensatory program. The educator cannot assume that if he avoids exotic words his students will understand his speech. He must be prepared to teach a process by which words are attached to their referents and to begin with objects and actions in the child's own environment. He must begin there not because this area is "familiar" to the child, but because in spite of its familiarity, it is not adequately coded in his language system. Furthermore, not only passive recognition of vocabulary should be taught, but also the active use of such vocabulary items.

## B. Category Formation

The literature on what has been called category formation, superordinate concept formation, and classification behavior lies in a disputed area between the study of semantics and the study of cognitive structures. Younger children, confronted with an array of objects — animals, dolls, kitchen utensils, and vehicles, for example — and asked to put the ones together that go together, tend to make mixed groupings (complexive groupings) which they justify by using "thematic" verbal explanations ("The lady drives the car"). Older children begin to use more consistent superordinate groupings, sometimes based on perceptual reasons ("They all have wheels"), sometimes on functional reasons ("You can cook with them all"), and sometimes on nominal reasons ("They are all animals"). This is a crude overview of trends with age subject to many qualifications, especially about the precise nature of the task employed and the materials used. However, this general trend has been observed by a number of investigators (Inhelder and Piaget, 1958, pp. 1-35; Annett, 1959, p. 234; Thompson, 1941, p. 123).

The role that language plays in the development of this ability is subject to a great deal of dispute. Vygotsky (1962, p. 59) and Bruner, Olver, and Greenfield (1966, pp. 30-67) argue that the child's ability to direct behaviorlike classification through language is the most advanced stage of intellectual development. Inhelder and Piaget give language an important but clearly secondary role in intellectual development, especially during the preschool years. With specific reference to classification, they state: ". . . we could give language no more than an auxiliary role (e.g., that of an accelerator). We might even say that while language is necessary for the completion of the structures, it is insufficient for their formation . . ." (Inhelder and Piaget, 1958, p. 2).

Piaget attributes the development of classification and of other cognitive abilities to the growth of intellectual operations, which are an elaboration of perceptual and motor schemas (Inhelder, 1966, p. 160). The testable implication of Piaget's position seems to be that no amount of linguistic training will accelerate the *appearance* of the ability to sort objects into consistent and exhaustive categories.

With this controversy in mind, it is important to note the precise nature of social class differences in such classification behavior. Sigel, Anderson, and Shapiro (1966, p. 6) studied middle- and lower-class children (ages three to five) on an object-sorting task employing familiar objects. He scores the reasons children give for making certain groupings as relational, descriptive, and categorical. He found more relational sortings in the lower-class subjects and more descriptive and categorical sortings in the middle class, thus suggesting that lower-class subjects operate on a developmentally less advanced level than middle-class children. Hess and Shipman (1965, p. 883) administered a sorting task to four-year-old children and employed a scoring scheme similar to Sigel's. In scoring the verbal responses of children from different social classes, they found more nonresponses and relational responses among lower-class children and more descriptive and categorical responses in the middle class.

John and Goldstein (1963, p. 271) scored the nonverbal responses (the sortings themselves) of children of different social class into true subordinate sortings vs. mixed sortings. They found no differences in these nonverbal scores at the first grade, but they did find differences at the fifth grade.

Hess and Shipman and Sigel find differences across social class for three- to five-year-olds on tasks where the quality of the verbal explanation is ranked on a developmental scale, while John finds no differences at the first grade on a nonverbal sorting task. Consistent with these findings are those of Kaplan and Mandel (1967, p. 10), who report significant social class differences among boys 6 to 12 in the quality of verbal reasons on a sorting task but no difference by social class on a nonverbal scoring of the sortings. The authors are not explicit about their scoring scheme or controls for social class.

The findings of Stodolsky (1965, pp. 41-55) are generally in accord with those cited above. Using a sorting task devised by Kohlberg, she was able to assign both a verbal and nonverbal score to the sortings of her five-year-old subjects. She found significant differences between her middle- and lower-lower-class subjects on both the verbal and nonverbal sorting scores, although differences were much greater on the verbal task. If one equates her "associative" grouping with the "thematic" grouping described earlier, the middle class employs proportionally more true category sortings and fewer relational groupings than the lower class on both the verbal and nonverbal task.

Thus, verbal differences are greater than nonverbal differences when young children from different social classes perform sorting tasks, and nonverbal differences are sometimes not observed. The verbal responses of middle-class children are more often superordinate reasons, while lower-class children often give a thematic verbal response or none at all.

Returning to the Bruner-Piaget dispute, one could accept Piaget's view that language is not the decisive mechanism of cognitive development and still argue strongly for training lower-class children in the language of superordinate category formation. For it appears that in children of the same age from different social classes, the basic operational structures are present (as exemplified by small or nonexistent differences in children's nonverbal sorting scores), while differences in the language used to describe such sortings is the major deficit that separates lower-class from middle-class children. If, on the other hand, Bruner's view is more correct, then such language training becomes even more important.

## C. Language Associated with Conservation and Nonconservation

The experiments of Piaget and his associates concerning conservation of volume provide more evidence about specific aspects of language performance than are associated with more advanced cognitive development. In an effort to test the hypothesis that specific language training would accelerate the time at which children acquired conservation, Sinclair, a student of Piaget, first distinguished three major differences between the language of children who possessed conservation in contrast to children who did not (reported in Inhelder, 1966, pp. 162-63). In a task where they were asked to describe the differences between objects and between sets of objects, she found that children with conservation used:

1. More relational terms ("That one is larger than that one," instead of "That one is big. That one is small").
2. More differentiated descriptions ("That one is thin," instead of "That one is little").
3. More coordinated descriptions of objects differing on two dimensions ("That one is longer, but it is thinner").

An attempt to train children without conservation in these verbal skills did not produce conservation. However, the training procedure used by Sinclair was inadequate. The children were taught to use the types of descriptions outlined above in a single session and in a highly structured situation. In contrast, the conservation task was a much freer situation in which no cues were given by the experimenter as to what types of language were appropriate. The significance of this shift in situations is made apparent by the training experiment of Bereiter and Engelmann (1966, p. 52). They found that it was ten weeks after improvements in language performance were observed in a structured situation that they transferred to an unstructured situation. Thus, Piaget's one-day training experiment was an inadequate test. The role of language as an accelerator of this cognitive task is still in question, but Sinclair has given us valuable information about specific characteristics of language use that are associated with more advanced cognitive functioning.

Although no tests for social class differences in the use of these types of description have been undertaken, it seems quite likely, on the basis of the work described in Section IV of this paper (Krauss and Rotter, 1968), that such differences would appear. Some specific but fragmentary support for this position comes from the observation of Bereiter (1968, p. 2) that lower-class children have trouble with what Sinclair has called "coordinated" descriptions. Specifically, he reports that lower-class children fail to see that coordinated descriptions like "tall and short" are inappropriate.

## VI. Additional Investigations

Several additional fields of study provide useful insights for the development of a compensatory language program, although they do not fit neatly into the major rubrics under which research has been considered thus far.

## A. Language Skills Associated with Success in Reading

Another way to approach the problem of designing a compensatory language curriculum is to ask what types of language skills are associated with success or difficulty in later schoolwork. The skill of reading is so central to any school program that there is little question that it is important to develop language performance which will form a basis for reading success.

Evidence that specific differences in the syntax and phonology of dialects may cause communication difficulties was examined earlier. Labov (1967, p. 161) presents specific evidence that a few such differences (e.g., the dropping of the "-ed") may cause reading difficulties. He found, for example, that the majority of Negro children in his sample were unable to recognize that in reading the sentence "I looked for him when I read his name," they should recognize that the "-ed" on "looked" signals that "read" should be past tense. If a preschool program is to prepare a child to face such problems in elementary school, it seems that the same type of approach that was suggested to overcome possible difficulties in students' verbal comprehension because of dialect differences should be employed; i.e., emphasis on comprehension of contrasts in standard English through extensive contact with a standard English speaker, without an attempt to change the child's own speech patterns.

Several investigators have studied the relationship between complexity of oral language use and reading success. Martin (1955, p. 170) failed to find any relationship between the complexity of children's language in a speech sample and success in reading at the first-grade level. Strickland (reported in Chall, 1967, p. 158) also failed to find a relation between the complexity of language and reading ability at the second-grade level but did find such a relationship at sixth grade. Consistent with Strickland's results is Loban's six-year longitudinal study of grade school children. Like the other investigators, he failed to find a significant relationship between complexity of oral language use and reading ability in grades one and two. However, he found an increasingly significant relationship in the next four grades. At sixth grade the oral language use of the children was an extremely significant prediction of both exceptional reading success and exceptional failure. Furthermore, Loban's longitudinal design allows him to conclude that those children who had the best oral language abilities at grade one are those who read best at grade six. This finding underscores the importance of early development of the types of oral language skills outlined in Sections IV and V.[3]

Finally, Chall (1967, p. 149) reports that the most important characteristic of preschool programs associated with success in beginning reading is training in the names and sounds of letters. Thus, these appear to be another important class of referents which should be taught in a compensatory language program.

## B. Direct Observation of Children

A number of investigators have commented that child development research has attempted to move to highly specific experimentation without first collecting broad observations of the total child in his own milieu (e.g., White, 1967). In this way, White argues, many obvious facts about development are overlooked. White's own preliminary results from the observation of preschool children contain several findings that are relevant to a compensatory language curriculum. He found that children generally classified as incompetent on a wide range of social and intellectual tasks lacked the "ability to get and maintain the attention of the teacher" and the "ability to use the teacher as a resource" (White, 1967, p. 15). Related to this observation is a finding of Tough (1969) that lower-class three-year-olds are less likely than their middle-class counterparts to ask questions that seek explanation.

Other observations specifically aimed at isolating language difficulties of lower-class children were undertaken by Bereiter and Engelmann (1966) and were used in developing the curriculum for their well-known training experiment. Their global summary of the language difficulties of lower-class children seems highly doubtful:

The speech of the severely deprived children seems to consist not of distinct words, as does the speech of middle-class children of the same age, but rather of whole phrases or sentences that function like giant

[3] Alternatively, it may be that the reading methods employed relied too heavily on oral language and that methods could be developed which would teach children with low oral language ability to read as well as those with high ability.

words. That is to say, these "giant word" units cannot be taken apart by the child and recombined; they cannot be transformed from statements to questions, from imperatives to declaratives, and so on. Instead of saying "He's a big dog," the deprived child says "He bih daw." Instead of saying "I ain't got no juice," he says "Uai-ga-na-ju." Instead of saying "That is a red truck," he says "Da-re-truh" (Bereiter and Engelmann, 1966, p. 34).

Bereiter's assertion that severely deprived children speak in "giant sentence words" is not supported by the evidence presented in his statement above. Although his rendition of sentences from his subjects may strike the average reader as extremely odd, closer inspection indicates that these sentences merely reflect minor syntactic and phonological contrasts between Negro dialect and standard English reviewed earlier, including omission of "be" and consonant-cluster simplification. For example, the difference between "That is a red truck" and "Da-re-truh" is the omission of the copulative "is" plus the weakening of the final consonants "t," "d," and "k."

Bereiter's assertion also runs counter to evidence presented earlier based on the data of Cazden (1965), Osser (1967), Shriner and Miner (1967), and Baratz (1968) that indicates no significant differences by race and social class in the development of the syntactic competence that allows children to substitute words in complex syntactic patterns.

It might be argued that results of Bereiter's observations differed from the results of other investigations because the children he observed were more severely deprived. In discussing this point, it is important to distinguish between his observation group and his experimental group. The experimental group members were chosen because an older sibling had suffered academic failure in school. Of the observational group, he says only that they consisted of 80 disadvantaged Negro preschool children, 30 of whom were observed intensively and 50 less intensively. Thus, there is no evidence that these children were any more severely deprived than the lower-class children tested in the studies reviewed earlier, most of whom were selected because of attendance in lower-class schools or in Head Start.

Finally, Bereiter's assertion runs counter to evidence summarized by Lenneberg (1967) which indicates that children in a wide variety of environmental circumstances acquire syntactic competence of the same type and at about the same rate, barring fairly severe brain damage or extreme isolation (e.g., the child who is kept in a closet for most of his life).

On the level of more specific deficiencies in lower-class language use, however, Bereiter and Engelmann provide a number of interesting observations. They find lower-class children:

1. Are unable to answer questions based on information provided in simple sentences. ("Puppies are baby dogs. What are puppies?")
2. Do not understand the meanings of prepositions and conjunctions like "or."
3. Do not understand logical negation. ("Show me something that is not red.")
4. Do not understand that phrases joined by "and" can be reversed. ("What's another way to say 'red and green'?")

One problem with these observations is that there are no data presented on social class differences in these language skills. They may be difficult for middle-class preschool children as well. However, like the observations of Sinclair (Inhelder, 1966), they provide possible further specification of specific language skills that might be included in a compensatory language program.

## VII. Summary of Language Skills Described So Far

Table I lists the language skills which have been judged thus far to be important ingredients in a compensatory language program. Although they have been derived from diverse perspectives on subcultural language differences, the skills listed seem to have a loose coherence and focus on what might be called the referential use of language. The use of an elaborated syntax is closely interdependent with the system of modification needed to express precise reference in spite of the cognitive demands of a communication situation. Also connected with an adequate reference system is the use of superordinate class names and ability to name common objects and actions.

A child able to employ these language skills could communicate

Table I. Language Skills for a Compensatory Language Program

| Skill | Investigator |
| --- | --- |
| A. Use of elaborated syntax: | |
| 1. complex verb phrases | Bernstein |
| 2. complex noun phrases | Loban; Tough |
| 3. subordination | Bernstein |
| 4. infinitives | Loban |
| B. Use of a precise language of reference: | |
| 1. detailed description of parts of stimuli | Krauss and Rotter |
| 2. modifiers which are relational, explicit, and coordinated | Inhelder |
| 3. pronouns with prior referents | Hawkins (in Cazden) |
| 4. vocabulary which describes familiar objects and actions | John; Lesser et al. |
| C. Use of superordinate class names | Stodolsky |
| D. Use of the following classes of words: | |
| 1. uncommon adjectives | Bernstein |
| 2. uncommon adverbs | Bernstein |
| 3. logical connectives | Bereiter |
| 4. negatives | Bereiter |
| E. Social: | |
| 1. ability to get and maintain teacher's attention | White |
| 2. ability to ask questions of teacher | Hess and Shipman |
| F. Ability to use information to give appropriate answers to questions | Bereiter |
| G. Reversal of conjoined words and phrases | Bereiter |
| H. Comprehension of contrasts between one's own speech and the standard dialect | |

a message with a minimum of dependence on gestures, previous knowledge shared with his listener, or dependence on visual props in the situation. Bruner has asserted that the most important ability acquired through schooling is the ability to "operate intellectually in the absence of a concrete situational context" (Bruner, Olver, and Greenfield, 1966, p. 316). The language skills in which we have observed subcultural differences seem to be closely associated with this ability. They should form the core of any compensatory language program that hopes to allow children to function in school without being handicapped by their social background.

## VIII. Teaching Situations

Although there is a paucity of evidence concerning the effectiveness of various teaching strategies and situations employed in preschool language programs, enough evidence exists so that specifically stated hypotheses can be framed that can be tested in training experiments. Again it is important to keep in mind the point made earlier that not all lower-class children (as designated by objective status indices) resemble group norms in terms of their language abilities. It is an empirical question as to which sorts of individuals within the lower-class group would profit from a given type of preschool language program. The following discussion applies with most force to those children who are fairly close to the norms for the lower-class group.

It seems profitable to distinguish between three general types of instructional situations: free-play situations with informal emphasis on verbal skills; training situations in which the teacher's response is made contingent on the child's; and training situations in which the child's response is made contingent on the teacher's.

### A. Informal Emphasis on Verbal Skills

The first situation is the one that predominates in most nursery school and Head Start programs. It has been transferred into programs for lower-class students from a nursery school movement which was developed essentially for middle-class children. An analysis of the cognitive and social demands of this situation makes it extremely unlikely that it facilitates the development of the skills outlined in Table I. With respect to cognitive demands, the situation seems quite similar to the middle-class home situations studied by Brown. Students and teachers probably use the same sort of vague referential language characteristic of this situation. With respect to social demands and characteristics of the situation, it seems to favor children who are capable of attracting and holding the teacher's attention, since the teacher sees herself as "helper" and assumes a passive role. As our earlier discussion of White's observations indicates, children who are capable of getting and holding the teacher's attention in such a situation are those likely to be the most advanced in intellectual development. In addition, previous discussion of the attitudes lower-class children bring to linguistic interaction with adults indicates that lower-class children are reluctant to take the verbal initiative with adults and are instructed to be passive in school by their mothers. Thus, those children who have the greatest need for verbal interaction with the teacher are probably those who communicate least; the less intellectually able are those children who have been socialized into the negative attitudes toward verbal interaction typical of lower-class child rearing.

There seems to be good empirical support for these speculations. Some protocols of children's speech in a typical Head Start free-play situation have been collected by the Institute for Developmental Studies of New York University. My preliminary analysis of these data indicates that these children almost never specify the subject of an utterance with a precise noun or noun phrase and that their sentences are grammatically simple. Furthermore, a substantial percentage of the verbal output of the child consists of stereotyped sentences and phrases. Here, for example, are the utterances of one boy during a five-minute sampling of his speech:

> Hey! Give me one. . . . You ate one. . . .
> Thow this away. . . . Throw this away. . . . Throw this away. . . .
> He, He talks like that. . . .
> Looky his feet. . . .
> Let me take one these. . . .
> Not me! Not me! . . .

Further negative evidence about the value of such situations for language development comes from Bereiter and Engelmann (1966, pp. 15-16). Reviewing the evidence on this type of compensatory program, they find no program that has brought lower-class children up to age norms on verbal skills.

### B. Teacher's Response Contingent on Students

An example of this type of teaching situation is Cazden's (1965) experiment on the effects of extension vs. expansion in children's syntactic development. According to transformational theory concerning syntactic development the child functions as a theory constructor with a great deal of preprogrammed processing equipment

(Chomsky, 1965, pp. 53-55). It has been suggested that the best way to facilitate syntactic development is to provide the child with a rich and varied sample of adult speech as raw materials for this theorizing. Cazden's (1965) results (in which the most effective language treatment was one in which the children's verbalizations were "extended" by the tutor) have been interpreted as supporting this argument. There is even some evidence that overt response is not necessary to syntactic development. Lenneberg (1962) reports the case of a child who developed quite sophisticated comprehension although he could not speak. Exact imitation of adult speech is considered valueless in syntactic development (Ervin, 1964, p. 172).

However, as was indicated earlier, the development of syntactic competence does not seem to be an area of significant social class differences. Children of different social classes do not seem to differ in important respects in the rules that comprise their competence or in the speed with which they acquire these rules. It appears, as Cazden concludes, that children's syntactic development does not seem to be sensitive to differences in the quality of mothers' speech (Cazden, 1967b, p. 15). Perhaps only a minimum level of speech stimulation, available to almost all children, is necessary for adequate syntactic development of basic grammatical rules.

However, as our review of the literature demonstrated, it is not possession of the basic rules in one's competence, but the appropriate use of these rules in particular situations and the elaboration of the basic rule to create more complex syntactic structures that seem to be the key to social class language differences that will have consequences for school situations. The extension situation and others in which the teacher's response is contingent seem to have some potential value in developing these skills of language use. The teacher should be able to set up the physical situation for such interactions in a way that will promote referential language use. Furthermore, sustained discourse with an adult in a tutorial situation should in itself promote more precise expression. Finally, since Cazden reports that many of her tutors' responses were questions, it seems that the tutor is still exercising a measure of control in the extension situation which could be directed toward developing the types of language skills outlined in Table I.

## C. Student Responses Shaped by Teacher

In a third type of situation, the teacher plays a more active shaping role, structuring the situation to elicit specific sentence types, modifiers, appropriate use of superordinate category names, and so forth. If, as I have argued, the most important general ability for the lower-class child to acquire is the ability to *use* a highly specific type of referential language in particular situations, this third type of training situation should be most effective in developing the specific prerequisite skills outlined in Table I. Bereiter and Engelmann (1966) have provided a model of such a program and have produced impressive evidence about gains in IQ and language skill of children who have participated in it.

A number of objections have been raised to this approach, and it is important to consider them briefly.

First, such a program involves a great deal of structured drill and repetition. Bereiter and Engelmann, for example, made extensive use of sentence imitation, much in the same way that pattern drills are used in teaching a foreign language. For those who object to such repetitive practice, Elkind's comments seem especially appropriate:

One of the features of cognitive growth that Piaget and Montessori observed and to which they both attached considerable importance, is the frequently repetitive character of behaviors associated with emerging mental abilities. Piaget and Montessori are almost unique in this regard since within both psychology and education repetitive behavior is often described pejoratively as "rote learning" or "perseveration." Indeed, the popular view is that repetition is bad and should be avoided in our dealings with children. What both Piaget and Montessori have recognized, however, is the very great role which repetitive behavior plays in mental growth (Elkind, 1967, pp. 541-42).

Thus, it appears that repetition that is done at a more leisurely pace by the middle-class child must be compressed into a shorter period in a compensatory program that is going to make a difference.

Second, it is inaccurate to maintain that the majority of responses in such a program need to be or should be pure rote. Tasks can be designed in which extremely sophisticated thinking is involved in spite of the fact that the teacher can anticipate what an acceptable response will be.

Third, and finally, the tone of Bereiter's and Engelmann's work suggests that the gains students in their program made can be accomplished only at the cost of repressive regimentation (e.g., they advise teachers to give unruly students a good shaking or lock them in a dark closet). It is certainly possible to set up a structured tutoring situation in which a warm relationship exists between student and teacher, in which there is a great deal of tolerance for diversions, and in which a portion of the total program is still devoted to other kinds of activity.

Handled in this way, and incorporating practice in the use of the language skills outlined in Table I, this third type of instructional situation seems the most effective one for teaching the grammatically elaborated and referentially precise language use that seems to be the major subcultural language deficit having adverse effects on the educability of preschool children.

## Summary

This paper has reviewed the literature on subcultural differences in language development to determine what this literature suggests about the nature of a language program for lower-class four-year-olds. This review reaches the following major conclusions:

1. That differences in syntactic and phonological competence are not important barriers to communication for the lower-class preschool child and should not be the focus of preschool language training.

2. That, of the many subcultural differences in language, the major difference which puts the average lower-class child at a *disadvantage* in the educational process is his relative lack of ability in using a precise language of description, especially in situations where (a) speakers cannot rely on previously shared information, (b) the speaker must specifically describe referents which are not perceptually present or about which the listener lacks information, and (c) the bulk of the communication load falls on the language code itself, as opposed to such extralinguistic activities as gesturing.

3. That the literature on subcultural differences in language use is

rich enough at this point to provide evidence of many of the specific language skills which comprise the use of this "abstract" type of language.

4. That the traditional preschool is not likely to foster the use of these specific language skills which the lower-class child needs most to master.

5. That of two broad types of more focused language intervention programs (one in which the teacher's response is contingent on the child's and one in which the child's response is contingent on the teacher's), the latter, more highly structured program will probably be more successful in teaching the crucial language skills.

All of these contentions are, of course, arguable at this point in time, since the most valuable types of evidence needed to settle questions concerning the nature of subcultural language differences in young children and the effectiveness of preschool language intervention do not exist. With respect to the issue of subcultural differences in syntactic competence, for example, we lack longitudinal studies of language development in children of different social classes. With respect to the effectiveness of language intervention programs, no more than a handful of carefully controlled language training experiments have ever been conducted in this country. The author is currently conducting a training experiment that attempts to assess the effect of teaching a precise language of referential description by the two major teaching methods analyzed in this paper (extension vs. pattern drill).

Continued research on subcultural language differences, coupled with constant attempts to translate these findings into language training experiments, will test the validity of the type of specific hypotheses advanced in this paper and other more refined ones that are put in their place.

## References

Annett, M. 1959. The classification of instances of four common class concepts by children and adults. *British Journal of Educational Psychology* 29: 223-36.

Baratz, J. C. 1968. A bi-dialectal test for determining language proficiency. Unpublished paper.

Barber, B. 1957. *Social stratification.* New York: Harcourt, Brace and Jovanovich.

Bellugi, U. 1966. The development of questions and negatives in the speech of three children. Special qualifying paper, Harvard Graduate School of Education.

Bellugi, U. 1967. The acquisition of the system of negation in children's speech. Doctoral dissertation, Harvard Graduate School of Education.

Bellugi-Klima, U. 1968. Grammatical comprehension tests. Unpublished paper.

Bereiter, C. 1968. Children's problems in coordinating language and reality. Paper presented at a conference on problems of teaching young children, University of Toronto.

Bereiter, C., and Engelmann, S. 1966. *Teaching disadvantaged children in the preschool.* Englewood Cliffs, N.J.: Prentice-Hall.

Berko, J. 1958. The child's learning of English morphology. *Word* 14: 150-77.

Bernstein, B. 1962a. Linguistic codes, hesitation phenomena and intelligence. *Language and Speech* 5: 1-13.

Bernstein, B. 1962b. Social class, linguistic codes and grammatical elements. *Language and Speech* 5: 221-40.

Bernstein, B. 1964. Aspects of language and learning in the genesis of the social process. In D. Hymes, ed., *Language in culture and society.* New York: Harper and Row, pp. 251-63.

Bernstein, B. 1965. A socio-linguistic approach to social learning. In J. Gould, ed., *Penguin survey of the social sciences.* Baltimore, Md.: Penguin, pp. 144-68.

Bernstein, B. 1967. Social structure, language and learning. In J. P. de Cecco, ed., *The psychology of language, thought and instruction.* New York: Holt, Rinehart and Winston.

Blau, P., and Duncan, O. 1967. *The American occupational structure.* New York: Wiley.

Bloom, B., Davis, A., and Hess, R. 1965. *Compensatory education for cultural deprivation.* New York: Holt, Rinehart, and Winston.

Brown, R., and Bellugi, U. 1964. Three processes in the child's acquisition of syntax. In E. Lenneberg, ed., *New directions in the study of language.* Cambridge, Mass.: MIT Press, pp. 131-61.

Brown, R., Cazden, C., and Bellugi-Klima, U. 1971. The child's grammar from I to III. In A. Bar-Adon and W. S. Leopold, eds., *Child language readings.* Englewood Cliffs, N.J.: Prentice-Hall.

Bruner, J., Olver, R., and Greenfield, P., eds. 1966. *Studies in cognitive growth.* New York: Wiley.

Cazden, C. 1965. Environmental assistance to the child's acquisition of grammar. Doctoral dissertation, Harvard University.

Cazden, C. 1966. Subcultural differences in child language: An interdisciplinary review. *Merrill-Palmer Quarterly* 12: 185-219.

Cazden, C. 1967a. Individual differences in language competence and performance. *Journal of Special Education* 2: 135-50.

Cazden, C. 1967b. The acquisition of noun and verb inflections. Unpublished manuscript.

Cazden, C. 1968. Three sociolinguistic views of the language and speech of lower class children — with special attention to the work of Basil Bernstein. *Developmental Medicine and Child Neurology* 10: 600-612.

Cazden, C. 1970a. The situation: A neglected source of social class differences in language use. *Journal of Social Issues* 26, no. 2: 35-59.

Cazden, C. 1970b. The neglected situation in child language research and education. In F. Williams, ed., *Language and poverty: Perspectives on a theme*. Chicago: Markham.

Chall, J. S. 1967. *Learning to read: The great debate*. New York: McGraw-Hill.

Cherry-Piesach, E. 1965. Children's comprehension of teacher and peer speech. *Child Development* 36: 467-80.

Chomsky, C. 1968. The acquisition of syntax in children from 5 to 10. Doctoral dissertation, Harvard University.

Chomsky, N. 1957. *Syntactic structures*. The Hague: Mouton and Co.

Chomsky, N. 1965. *Aspects of the theory of syntax*. Cambridge, Mass.: MIT Press.

Chomsky, N. 1966. *Topics in the theory of generative grammar*. The Hague: Mouton and Co.

Cohen, P. 1966. Some methods in sociolinguistic research. Paper presented at the Research Planning Conference on Language Development in Disadvantaged Children, Yeshiva University.

Coleman, J., et al. 1966. *Equality of educational opportunity*. Washington, D.C.: U.S. Department of Health, Education, and Welfare, Office of Education.

Deutsch, M., et al. 1967. *The disadvantaged child*. New York: Basic Books.

Elkind, D. 1967. Piaget and Montessori. *Harvard Educational Review* 37: 535-47.

Ervin, Susan M. 1964. Imitation and structural change in children's language. In E. Lenneberg, ed., *New directions in the study of language*. Cambridge, Mass.: MIT Press, pp. 163-89.

Ervin-Tripp, S. 1967. Sociolinguistics. Unpublished paper.

Ervin-Tripp, S., and Slobin, D. 1966. Psycholinguistics. *Annual Review of Psychology* 17: 435-74.

Ferguson, C. 1964. Diglossia. In D. Hymes, ed., *Language in culture and society*. New York: Harper and Row, pp. 429-39.

Gumperz, J. 1964. Linguistic and social interaction in two communities. In J. Gumperz and D. Hymes, eds., The ethnography of communication. Special publication of *American Anthropologist* 66 (6), pt. 2: 137-53.

Halle, M. 1964. Phonology in generative grammar. In J. Fodor and J. Katz, eds., *The structure of language*. Englewood Cliffs, N.J.: Prentice-Hall, pp. 334-52.

Hawkins, P. R. 1969. Social class, the nominal group and reference. *Language and Speech* 12, pt. 2: 125-35.

Heider, E. 1968. Style and effectiveness of children's verbal communications within and between social classes. Doctoral dissertation, Harvard University.

Hess, R., and Shipman, V. 1965. Early experience and the socialization of cognitive modes in children. *Child Development* 36: 869-86.

Hollingshead, S., and Redlich, F. 1958. *Social class and mental illness*. New York: Wiley.

Hymes, D. 1964a. Directions in (ethno) linguistic theory. In A. K. Romney and R. G. D'Andrade, eds., Transcultural studies in cognition. Special publication of *American Anthropologist* 66 (3), pt. 2: 6-56.

Hymes, D. 1964b. Introduction: Toward ethnographies of communication. In J. J. Gumperz and D. Hymes, eds., The ethnography of communication. Special publication of *American Anthropologist* 66 (6), pt. 2: 1-34.

Hymes, D. 1966. On communicative competence. Paper presented at the Research Planning Conference on Language Development in Disadvantaged Children, Yeshiva University.

Hymes, D. 1967. A model of the interaction of language and social setting. *Social Issues* 23: 8-28.

Inhelder, B., and Piaget, J. 1958. *The growth of logical thinking from childhood to adolescence*. New York: Basic Books.

Inhelder, B., et al. 1966. On cognitive development. *American Psychologist* 21: 160-64.

John, V. 1967. Communicative competence of low-income children: Assumptions and programs. Report to the Ford Foundation.

John, V., and Goldstein, L. 1963. The social context of language acquisition. *Merrill-Palmer Quarterly* 10: 265-75.

Kahl, J., and Davis, K. 1953. *The American class structure*. New York: Holt, Rinehart and Winston.

Kaplan, M., and Mandel, S. 1967. Age and social class factors in children's conceptual development. Paper read at Society for Research in Child Development.

Katz, J., and Postal, P. 1964. *An integrated theory of linguistic descriptions*. Cambridge, Mass.: MIT Press.

Klima, E. 1964a. Negation in English. In J. Fodor and J. Katz, eds., *The structure of language*. Englewood Cliffs, N.J.: Prentice-Hall, pp. 246-323.

Klima, E. 1964b. Relatedness between grammatical systems. *Language* 40: 1-20.

Krauss, R., and Rotter, G. 1968. Communication abilities of children as a function of age and status. *Merrill-Palmer Quarterly* 14: 161-73.

Labov, W. 1965. Stages in the acquisition of standard English. In R. Shuy, ed., *Social dialects and language learning*. Champaign, Ill.: National Council of Teachers of English, pp. 77-103.

Labov, W. 1967. Some sources of reading problems for Negro speakers of nonstandard English. In Frazier, ed., *New directions in elementary English*. Champaign, Ill.: National Council of Teachers of English, pp. 140-67.

Labov, W., et al. 1968. A study of the non-standard English of Negro and Puerto Rican speakers in New York City, Vol. 1. Unpublished manuscript.

Labov, W., and Cohen, P. 1966. Systematic relations of standard and nonstandard rules in the grammars of Negro speakers. *Project Literacy Reports* 8: 66-84.

Lawton, D. 1964. Social class language differences in group discussions. *Language and Speech* 7: 183-204.

Lenneberg, E. 1962. Understanding language without ability to speak: A case report. *Journal of Abnormal and Social Psychology* 65: 419-25.

Lenneberg, E. 1967. *Biological foundations of language.* New York: Wiley.

Lesser, G. S., Fifer, G., and Clark, D. H. 1965. Mental abilities of children in different social and cultural groups. *Monographs of the Society for Research in Child Development* 30 (4), Serial No. 102.

Lin, S. 1965. Pattern practice in the teaching of standard English to students with a non-standard dialect. New York: Teachers College, Bureau of Publications.

Loban, W. 1963. *The language of elementary school children.* Champaign, Ill.: National Council of Teachers of English.

Loban, W. 1966. *Problems in oral English.* Champaign, Ill.: National Council of Teachers of English.

Macnamara, J. 1967. Bilingualism in the modern world. *Social Issues* 23: 1-7.

Martin, C. 1955. Developmental relationships among language variables in the first grade. *Elementary English* 32: 167-71.

Miller, G., and McNeill, D. 1969. Psycholinguistics. In G. Lindzey and E. Aronson, eds., *Handbook of social psychology,* 2nd ed., Vol. 3. Reading, Mass.: Addison-Wesley, pp. 666-794.

Moore, D. 1968. Competence and performance factors in the development of copulative sentences in children of different social classes. Unpublished paper.

New York City Board of Education. 1968. *Nonstandard dialect.* Champaign, Ill.: National Council of Teachers of English.

Osser, H., et al. 1967. A study of the communicative abilities of disadvantaged children. Unpublished paper.

Osser, H., Wang, M., and Zaid, F. 1969. The young child's ability to imitate and comprehend speech: A comparison of two subcultural groups. *Child Development* 40: 1063-75.

Pederson, L. 1964. Non-standard Negro speech in Chicago. In W. A. Stewart, ed., *Non-standard speech and the teaching of English.* Washington, D.C.: Center for Applied Linguistics, pp. 16-23.

Rosenbaum, P. 1965. *A grammar of English predicate constructions.* Doctoral dissertation, MIT.

Schatzman, L., and Strauss, A. 1955. Social class and modes of communication. *American Journal of Sociology* 60: 329-38.

Shriner, T. H., and Miner, L. 1967. Morphological structures in the language of advantaged and disadvantaged children. Unpublished paper.

Sigel, I. E., Anderson, L. M., and Shapiro, H. 1966. Categorization behavior of lower- and middle-class Negro preschool children: Differences in dealing with representation of familiar objects. *Journal of Negro Education* 35: 218-29.

Slobin, D. I. 1968. Questions of language development in cross-cultural perspective. Unpublished manuscript.

Stewart, W. A. 1965. Urban Negro speech: Sociolinguistic factors affecting English teaching. In R. W. Shuy, ed., *Social dialects and language learning.* Champaign, Ill.: National Council of Teachers of English, pp. 10-18.

Stewart, W. A. 1966. Social dialect. Paper presented at the Research Planning Conference on Language Development in Disadvantaged Children, Yeshiva University.

Stodolsky, S. 1965. Maternal behavior and language concept formation in Negro preschool children: An inquiry into process. Doctoral dissertation, University of Chicago.

Templin, M. 1957. *Certain language skills in children: Their development and inter-relationships.* Minneapolis, Minn.: University of Minnesota Press.

Thompson, J. 1941. Ability of children of different grade levels to generalize on sorting tasks. *Journal of Psychology* 11: 119-26.

Tough, J. 1969. Language and environment: An interim report on a longitudinal study. Leeds, England: University of Leeds Institute of Education. Mimeographed.

Vygotsky, L. 1962. *Thought and language.* Cambridge, Mass.: MIT Press.

Warner, W., and Lunt, P. 1941. *The social life of a modern community.* New Haven, Conn.: Yale University Press.

Warner, W., et al. 1949. *Democracy in Jonesville.* New York: Harper.

White, B. 1967. A drawing board approach to early education. Unpublished address.

Williamson, J. 1965. Report on proposed study of the speech of Negro high school students in Memphis. In R. W. Shuy, ed., *Social dialects and language learning.* Champaign, Ill.: National Council of Teachers of English, pp. 23-27.

Wilson, A. 1967. Educational consequences of segregation in a California community. In U.S. Civil Rights Commission, *Racial isolation in the public schools.* Washington, D.C.: Government Printing Office, 2: 165-207.

Young, F. 1941. An analysis of certain variables in a developmental study of language. *Genetic Psychology Monographs* 23: 3-141.

# 2

WILBUR A. HASS

# On the Heterogeneity of Psychological Processes in Syntactic Development[1]

The study of children's language acquisition has a long and vener-
able history in psychology, including both relatively informal observations (Stern and Stern, 1928) and highly quantified tabulations
(McCarthy, 1954). Recently the area has been revitalized by
advances in linguistics and in developmental psychology. Linguistics
has contributed techniques for describing the incredibly interwoven
structures which comprise the adult's knowledge of a language
(Fodor and Katz, 1964; Langacker, 1968). This is reflected in
grammars of English which look quite different from the ones we
used in grammar school (e.g., Jacobs and Rosenbaum, 1968;
Langendoen, 1969). Developmental psychology has contributed
techniques for describing how psychological processes become re-
organized· as the child grows up. One way of portraying the
Piagetian revolution is in terms of a graded description of how a
person may do very similar things with quite different psychological
bases. These two contributions are coming together in *developmental
psycholinguistics,* which is exploring how they mutually illuminate
each other (McNeill, 1966; Sinclair-de-Zwart, 1969). Developmental psycholinguistics should be relevant to the practices of early

[1] An earlier version of this paper was presented at the A.E.R.A. Convention,
Los Angeles, February 1969, as part of a symposium on the National Laboratory
on Early Childhood Education. Preparation of the paper was supported by a
grant from the U.S. Office of Education to the Early Education Research Center
of the University of Chicago. The author is now at Shimer College, Mt. Carroll,
Illinois.

49

education (whether or not it is intended to be compensatory). This paper attempts to characterize certain points of relevance in the area of syntax.

## Characterizing the Child's Language

Developmental psycholinguistics arose out of a methodological insight; namely, that a child's utterances should be examined as if they were a corpus from an exotic language. That is to say, one should be careful of reading into them more structure than is required to account for what is actually observable. In particular, one must be careful not to assume that they have the structural features of the language of surrounding adults. This procedural principle is more than just a scientist's whimsical purism; it leads one to look at what the child is doing from another point of view. A young American child has more in the way of language than a slightly incomplete and inaccurate version of English; he has a way of dealing with language which is general and abstract. To focus on some feature of his language as "bad" English is to miss the point that that feature plays a definite role in his language structure and shows the processes he is bringing to bear in working on language. Phrased along these lines, language development is seen as a process of change in the child's organization of his language processing operations; this, far more than the elimination of specific mistakes, is what the normal child seems to be doing as he acquires his native language.

Investigators who have studied the naturalistic observations collected by the projects led by Roger Brown and Susan Ervin-Tripp (Bellugi and Brown, 1964; McNeill, 1966) have been amazed at the young child's ability to get to the heart of language structure. In trying to characterize this ability, typical of the members of the human race, investigators have sometimes been driven to paradoxical statements. Thus, David McNeill was forced to characterize his presentation to a conference of early educators at Yeshiva by saying that "the problem of acquiring a language does not exist" (Gordon, 1966, p. 36). Such presentations have usually included implications or statements that the very young child already knows what is most essential about language and that individual differences in this respect are minimal, probably not directly related to the environmental conditions of the child. Is it any wonder that such presentations have aroused considerable puzzlement and frustration in those who wish to assist language development through early education?

The point is that children's language contains a good deal of organization — organization which we as adults are likely to ignore if we approach a child and are struck by the fact that he phrases something he says in a "queer" way. And this point is similar in nature to the ones made by linguists in describing primitive languages and by Piagetians in describing the child's "lack of logic."

## Developmental Change in Language Structure

The organization of children's language *does* undergo change as children get older. If one follows a certain type of construction throughout the preschool years, as Bellugi did for negation in her doctoral dissertation (1967), a vivid series of sequenced stages appears. These are related to more general reorganizations in the shape of the child's grammar (Brown, Cazden, and Bellugi-Klima, 1971). This sort of information should be of direct use in planning and evaluating early education programs. It tells one where syntactic change is likely to be occurring for a given child or for children of a given age.

But we can aim for additional goals; we can strive to indicate not only *what* syntactic constructions are suitable for early education, but also *why* those constructions admit of change. Let me indicate what I have in mind through an example. We know that interesting things happen in the preschool years from the use of initial word combinations and throughout the school years from the use of adjectives to modify nouns. What is involved in the changes in such noun phrases? What is it about a child's functioning that is altered as the form of his language changes? We know enough about the structure of language now to be able to infer, with some specificity, that *three types of processes* may be at work in the production of elaborated noun phrases.

The first type of process parallels surface syntactic structure, which is familiar to most readers. Surface syntactic structure is

characterized by the familiar branching-tree structure which divides
a sentence into its major constituents, and each of these constituents
into *its* constituents, until individual meaning units about the size
of words are reached. The relevant psychological processes here are
ones of scheduling language as it proceeds in time; through these
techniques one can "keep one's place" in the speech stream as one
talks or listens. Noun phrases are interesting in this regard in English
because they may involve a good deal of left-branching; if one has a
phrase like "the fine old stone houses," one has to keep in mind
that "fine" goes with "houses" even though a number of other
words may intervene. The speaker of English must develop schemas
that react to "the fine old stone houses" as all right, but to "the
stone old fine houses" as odd — as just not *sounding* right. Properties which such perceptual-motor schemas must have are described
by Lashley (1951) and Yngve (1960).

Second, there is the matter of deep structure. It is not enough
just to know if a noun phrase "sounds right"; one must also know
how it can be used to refer to something in the world. The linguistic
techniques for describing the propositional content of phrases and
sentences are under a good deal of debate; no one formulation would
suit very many (Chomsky, in preparation; Bach, 1968; McCawley,
1968). In terms of psychology we are on the familiar, if not precisely
formulated, ground of symbolization. Thus, English adjectives, to
continue with our example, usually attribute some property to the
nouns they modify. Bound up with the use of such noun phrases is
the cognizing of a world organized along property vs. entity lines.
Not only that, but different subclasses of English adjectives differ
in the sorts of properties they denote, so that the property-space is
not a homogeneous one.

Still a third sort of factor is given recognition in syntactic transformations. Actually, what is involved here, in terms of linguistic
structure, is more correctly described as the particular organization
of deep structure which leads some transformations, but not others,
to be applicable. This sounds hopelessly complicated, but the phenomenon is a widespread one. Think, for instance, of the relation
between "stone houses," "houses of stone," and "houses which are
made out of stone." The closest psychological parallel here is the

process by which one packages the referential content into a "wording" which fits into the communicational setting, a technique for relating what it is that we are talking about to the situation in which the talking is actually going on. Thus, "the stone houses are old" and "the old houses are made out of stone" don't differ in what they are about — namely, some houses which are old and which are made out of stone — but they arrange that content so that one or the other of the properties is made more salient. Different types of transformations involve the speaker's stance toward what he is saying (asserting, denying, questioning, etc.), the conveying of emphasis, the adjustment in terms of who the speaker is and when he is speaking, and the paring off of redundancies and irrelevancies, among other things. What processes are carried out here are clearly related to social psychological formulations of role theory.

The point of what has just been said is that, for any grammatical construction one cares to look at, there are at least three ways of viewing it and relating its use to psychological processes. The implication for language programs in early education is that one must examine not only whether a certain construction can be produced or understood by a child, but how one or more of these three aspects of processing language can be facilitated. With this ideal in mind, we can take each of the three aspects of grammar, mentioned above, and briefly examine each with respect to three issues: (a) what characterizes developmentally more advanced functioning in terms of that aspect; (b) how may developmentally more advanced functioning be facilitated, given our understanding of the psychological nature of that aspect; and (c) can the facilitation of developmentally more advanced functioning in that aspect be expected to lead to general cognitive benefits?

## Surface Syntactic Structure

How does this develop? Some ways are readily recognized in the most commonplace measures of language: increase in number of terminal elements (vocabulary size), increase in number of terminal elements included within syntactic organization (sentence length), and so on. Sometimes a process of subdivision of terminal units apparently takes place; what has been a single unit for a child becomes a "phrase." The process of refinement and decontextualizing of surface syntactic categories seems to continue throughout childhood.

Socioeconomically disadvantaged children are probably somewhat low on most such indices one might devise. However, a more striking fact is that such children do have a rich surface structure, which is sometimes indistinguishable on current measures from that of middle-class children. Attempts to do language training in this area have usually been in the direction of altering a few superficial differences between the dialect of the child and more standard American dialect. Attempts at early education, either of the "linguistic cosmetics" sort just mentioned or of more broad-gauged efforts to improve general parameters of surface syntactic structure, are best fashioned along the lines of instruction in perceptual-motor skills. The primary curricular problem is securing enough drill which is engrossing enough so that the child will approach it with some enthusiasm. The possibilities for general cognitive facilitation from such practice are approximately parallel to those for expecting increase in IQ from learning how to swim with a butterfly stroke. I say "approximately parallel" because children probably tend to read transformational and deep structural relevance into language even when no cues have been provided in the training process.

## Deep Structure

Despite disagreement on the exact form of descriptions of deep structure, and therefore on the representation of developmental change in deep structure, what is relevant here is the change in the way the child organizes the symbolic content of his language. Such change must be closely tied in with all that we know about cognitive development. Accordingly, changes like those in transposition and reversal shift (as studied by experimental child psychologists), to say nothing of Piagetian tasks relevant to the establishment of concrete operations, should be paralleled in the organization of deep structure. One should not, for instance, assign semantic markers to a child's system unless one has reason to believe that he does indeed treat the marker in question as a bipolar dimension. The establishment of how children handle such semantic dimensions and relations is essential in describing the form of their meaning system. A simple paradigm here would be the syntagmatic-paradigmatic shift in word association, which needs to be studied with additional variations. The status of socioeconomically disadvantaged children in these respects can hardly be settled at present. Presumably, at least as a makeshift, one can rely on referential cues in the language situation to be of value in the early education of deep structure; what one ultimately wants, of course, is for the child to be able to talk about things that are not present in the here-and-now.

Concern with modification of deep structure is evident in Carl Bereiter's program (Bereiter and Engelmann, 1966). I agree with his implication that changes in a person's deep structure can hardly fail to be related to his general way of thinking about things, since by definition deep structure is that aspect of language tied up with semantic interpretation. What I have reservations about in Bereiter's rationale is the assumption that deep-structure features are directly mapped onto surface structure. That this relation is, instead, most indirect has been demonstrated by the cumulative revisions in transformational linguistic theory. For any semantic content one might propose, there are several very different ways that it may be expressed in surface structure as well as vice versa. What psychological rationale can be given for this indirectness? As mentioned above, we have in mind the evolution of language to fit into interpersonal communicational settings and the concurrent transformational "packaging devices." In artificial languages, like the logics to which Bereiter refers, such devices have been eliminated as nearly as possible. To teach a child such a logic might be of some value, but it is not training in the full potentiality of natural language.

## Transformations

There is evidence from Roger Brown's data that, at least in the early stages of language development, the number of transformations that can be performed by a child does increase (Brown and Hanlon, 1968). Whether there is additional ordering in terms of which types of transformations come before which other ones is not certain. A large number of studies *have* shown that as children get older, they get better at describing objects in ways that enable others to determine what they are talking about — at adjusting their language to fit the communication situation. Socioeconomically disadvantaged children are particularly poor at such tasks; this "communicational egocentrism" on their part is, I believe, only one sample of the relative paucity of transformational processes in young disadvantaged children.

How can transformational processes best be taught? Procedures can be developed, in line with G. H. Mead's stress on reciprocity in role relations, since a major aspect of transformational functioning derives from taking the role of the other. This point is obviously related to Basil Bernstein's (1965) hypothesis that children with few and rigid role relations should have "restricted" language. At any rate, transformational processes are bound up with situations in which speakers take complementary and interchanging stances toward whatever it is that they are talking about. This requires not merely labeling drill but situations in which both speaker and listener have serious communicational intent — i.e., they really have something to say to each other. Exactly how to shape such interaction toward particular goals in language curriculums in early education critically needs attention.

When such transformationally related processes are a part of early education, they seem to go hand in hand with more general role-taking skills, as may be inferred from Flavell (1968). The expected benefits from such a program are not synonymous with good social adjustment, as witness the communicational skills of the con man. But the relevant cognitive benefits should be peculiarly social and personal in nature; while training in deep structure might lead to the development of language *about* human beings (if that were the content emphasized), transformational training would be directed toward the development of language *with* human beings.

## The Developing Nature of Language Rules

The whole matter of language training in early education is made even more complicated by the overall change, as the child grows up, in the sense in which he may be said to "have" language rules of any sort. A two-year-old may have regular patterns of word combination, and one may speak of these as exemplifying his "rules." But such rules are far different, psychologically, from the self-conscious rules of the adolescent. One cannot imagine how to find out if the two-year-old thinks of syntactic rules as inherent in language, as regulated by society, or as matters of personal language sense — but these are quite natural matters to inquire into once he gets somewhat older. One would expect that the child's conception of rules of language would follow the general Piagetian trends as do his ideas about rules of other sorts. How the status of rule concepts interacts with the various aspects of language mentioned above, in the period when operationality is coming into being (that is, the period when we attempt early education), deserves to be investigated in its own right.

## Conclusion

What are the implications for the design of language curriculums of the picture of language development that has just been painted? Currently established programs combine the aspects we have discussed in various unsystematic ways (Brottman, 1968). Thus, if one sees change in the use of a certain grammatical construction by a child, one has no way of knowing whether one has affected processes related to surface structure, deep structure, and/or transformations. These shotgun approaches are the best one can do at present; in order to try to get change in language, one puts everything that looks promising into the training program. Ultimately, we may look forward to the design of syntactic rifles — programs which are directed toward a certain process which seems to be particularly underdeveloped in the children with whom one is working. One would expect a quite different sort of program for bilingual children than for disadvantaged children, and a somewhat different program for black urban slum children than for Appalachian children. Whether we would expect general cognitive facilitation from the program would be a function of the particular features that had been included in it. If this paper has made the reader suspicious of global statements on the influence of language training on cognition, it has achieved its major goal.

## References

Bach, E. 1968. Nouns and noun phrases. In E. Bach and R. T. Harms, eds., *Universals in linguistic theory*. New York: Holt, Rinehart, and Winston, pp. 90-122.

Bellugi, U. 1967. The acquisition of the system of negation in children's speech. Doctoral dissertation, Harvard Graduate School of Education.

Bellugi, U., and Brown R., eds. 1964. The acquisition of language. *Monographs of the Society for Research in Child Development* 29 (1).

Bereiter, C., and Engelmann, S. 1966. *Teaching disadvantaged children in the preschool*. Englewood Cliffs, N.J.: Prentice-Hall.

Bernstein, B. 1965. A socio-linguistic approach to social learning. In J. Gould, ed., *Penguin survey of the social sciences*. London: Penguin, pp. 144-68.

Brottman, M. A., ed. 1968. Language remediation for the disadvantaged preschool child. *Monographs of the Society for Research in Child Development* 33 (8).

Brown, R., Cazden, C., and Bellugi-Klima, U. 1971. The child's grammar from I to III. In A. Bar-Adon and W. S. Leopold, eds., *Child language readings*. Englewood Cliffs, N.J.: Prentice-Hall.

Brown, R., and Hanlon, C. 1968. Derivational complexity and order of acquisition in child speech. Paper given at Carnegie-Mellon Symposium on Cognition, Pittsburgh, Pa.

Chomsky, N. In preparation. Remarks on nominalizations.

Flavell, J. H. 1968. *The development of role-taking and communication skills in children*. New York: Wiley.

Fodor, J., and Katz, J., eds. 1964. *The structure of language*. Englewood Cliffs, N.J.: Prentice-Hall.

Gordon, E., ed. 1966. *Research planning conference on language development in disadvantaged children*. New York: Ferkauf Graduate School of Education, Yeshiva University.

Jacobs, R. A., and Rosenbaum, P. S. 1968. *English transformational grammar*. Waltham, Mass.: Blaisdell.

Langacker, R. W. 1968. *Language and its structure*. New York: Harcourt, Brace and World.

Langendoen, D. T. 1969. *The study of syntax*. New York: Holt, Rinehart, and Winston.

Lashley, K. S. 1951. The problem of serial order in behavior. In L. A. Jeffress, ed., *Cerebral mechanisms in behavior*. New York: Wiley.

McCarthy, D. 1954. Language development in children. In L. Carmichael, ed., *Manual of child psychology*. New York: Wiley, pp. 492-630.

McCawley, J. D. 1968. The role of semantics in grammar. In E. Bach and R. T. Harms, eds., *Universals in linguistic theory*. New York: Holt, Rinehart, and Winston, pp. 124-69.

McNeill, D. 1966. Developmental psycholinguistics. In F. Smith and G. A. Miller, eds., *The genesis of language*. Cambridge, Mass.: MIT Press, pp. 15-84.

Sinclair-de-Zwart, H. 1969. Developmental psycholinguistics. In D. Elkind and J. H. Flavell, eds., *Studies in cognitive development: Essays in honor of Jean Piaget*. New York: Oxford University Press, pp. 315-36.

Stern, C., and Stern, W. 1928. *Die kindersprache*. 4th ed. Leipzig: Barth.

Yngve, V. 1960. A model and an hypothesis for language structure. *Proceedings of the American Philosophical Society* 104: 444-66.

# 3

IRVING SIGEL

# Language of the Disadvantaged: The Distancing Hypothesis[1]

The argument in this paper is based on the fundamental premise that the ostensive world is one of three dimensions where objects (animate and inanimate) are perceived in their solidity and depth either as instigators of actions or as recipients of actions. It is this ostensive environment in all its complexity and diversity that becomes transformed (reconstructed) into mental or symbolic representations; e.g., images, pictures, etc. These representations furnish data which are stored and/or utilized in the course of building classifications. This brings us to the central theme; namely, the process and conditions involved in transforming the three-dimensional environment into its representations. For example, how does the individual learn to recognize or realize that the three-dimensional world can be represented in *two* dimensions?

Representations are acquired initially and perhaps all through life in the course of interactions with three-dimensional reality. These

[1] An earlier version of this paper, under the title "The Distancing Hypothesis: A Casual Hypothesis for the Acquisition of Representable Thought," was presented at the symposium on The Effects of Early Experience, University of Miami, December 1968, Marshall R. Jones, Ph.D., Chairman.

I wish to thank Miss Joan Bliss, University of Geneva; Dr. Marjorie Franklin, Bank Street College; and Dr. William Overton, State University of New York at Buffalo, for their careful reading of the manuscript and their advice in helping reduce conceptual confusion and obscurantism in this paper. Failure to achieve this reduction is my responsibility. Dr. Franklin helped stimulate the discussion on language.

Some of the research reported in this paper was funded by Office of Economic Opportunity Contracts #542, #1410, and #4118.

representations form bases for action in lieu of the presence of the realities; e.g., responses to pictures which are derivatives or generalizations or equivalents to that three-dimensional reality. The child responds to his mother and to a picture of his mother with full knowledge that the latter is a representation of his mother. The recognition that the picture is a representation (i.e., stands for or in place of the mother) is a significant developmental accomplishment. We do not yet know how the child comes to this awareness. How does he learn that objects and events can be represented with fewer dimensions?

*How* man thinks, *what* man remembers, *what* man perceives, *what* man does with the knowledge that he acquires are derivatives of and dependent on man's basic capability to represent the world mentally. We tend to take for granted that ability to deal with the world representationally is a "given." In so much of our psychological research we assume that the subjects are all functioning at a representational level. For example, most of the experimental stimuli employed in research in perception, in learning, in memory, and in thinking are re-presented material. Pictures, sounds, various kinds of visual stimuli of a graphic order, all of these are the stimuli to which the organism is asked to react. Our measures of intelligence for the most part contain graphic symbols. In effect, studies employ representations or graphisms, and therefore it is to that reality our subjects respond. Is it not ironic that much of what we know about cognition is based on response systems to representations? Yet we know little about this first step. It is as though we start in the midst of the behavioral stream. Undergirding all these response capabilities is the accepted idea that the individual has the capability to respond to representational stimuli.

I shall present an array of data, from a variety of sources, which clearly shatters the assumption that man "naturally" responds to representation, that children automatically have the response repertoire by which to evoke or employ representational thought, even with stimuli as presumably simple as photographs of familiar objects. In this paper I will show that children's ability to deal with representations of their environment is indeed a function of life experiences and will vary accordingly.

## Some Data on Representational Competence

Turning to the data upon which these assertions are based, I will begin with a study I reported in 1953. At that time I reported that lower-middle-class boys with average mental ability, when asked to classify familiar items, employed similar categories for classification irrespective of the level of symbolization of the stimuli (Sigel, 1953). Free-sorting tasks were used, employing three-dimensional toys, black and white pictures of these toys, and words (names of the items). The items used were in the following categories: vehicles, furniture, animals, and people. The results of this study indicated that the boys, irrespective of age and level of representation, tended to use similar kinds of classification. I concluded, therefore, that the level of representation (i.e., the object, picture, or word) was not a necessary relevant dimension for these boys, aged 7, 9, and 11. The relevant dimension was the meaning which transcended the physical or graphic representation of the object. To put it another way, the meaning attributed to an object was not altered by alteration of the mode of representing that object (Sigel, 1954). The intrinsic meaning of the object is conserved (i.e., is maintained) in the face of transformations, and the child is not confused by variations in the mode of representation. The ability of the child to respond in such a consistent manner is designated as *representational competence;* i.e., the ability to deal competently and equivalently with representational material.

Many years later, when I resumed work in cognitive styles, I decided to pretest some black and white photographs of familiar items in order to create a sorting task. The only school available contained the age groups we needed (namely, children five and six) but was predominantly a lower-class black school. We assumed, in view of our previous research, that the social class might not really be a very relevant variable; so I blithely proceeded to present my black and white pictures in the usual format to these children and discovered they had difficulty classifying the pictures. They tended to associate them by chaining, frequently thematically rather than on the basis of class membership or common properties. Items selected tended to bear little or no functional relationship to previous or subsequent choices. A typical performance would be one in which the child selects a picture of an object and then chooses a second one as related to the first, but a third choice is not selected as related to the first. Why did these children tend to have such difficulty in simple free-classification tasks? Two questions come to mind: (a) do these children lack the skills needed for classifying objects, or (b) do these children have difficulty because the stimuli are pictures? I was inclined to reject this second question for the following reasons: (a) the children were able to label the items in each picture correctly; and (b) since the results of the earlier study showed no differences in classification, I had no reason to believe that the mode of representation was at issue. Rather, I was inclined to think that these children lacked the capability to abstract, in this sense, to search for commonalities, and to build classes. An astute kindergarten teacher quickly disabused me of this notion when she said that the correct labeling of the picture does not necessarily indicate the child understands that picture. The children could not group pictures, she explained, because they lacked the awareness that the picture was in fact a representation. It disturbed me to receive such a sophisticated answer from the teacher. Why could we not have thought of this? Such wisdom is frequently overlooked by researchers. Believing that the teacher was dead wrong, but with a nagging doubt regarding my own judgment, I decided it was necessary to repeat the format of the earlier classification studies with lower-class children, using three-dimensional objects and their two-dimensional counterparts. In essence, I replicated the 1953 study. For a more stringent comparison between "real" and representation, I decided to use three-dimensional life-sized objects instead of toys, since toys are actually representations.

Two sorting tasks were created containing three-dimensional life-sized objects, each familiar to lower- and middle-class children (e.g., cup, pencil, pipe, etc.), and two-dimensional colored photographs of these objects blown up to approximate as closely as possible the size and color of the objects.

A number of studies were done comparing group performance with the two- and three-dimensional tasks. The results revealed that the teacher was indeed right; the mode of representation of the items posed a problem for the children. The grouping of three-dimensional objects by lower-class children did not differ significantly from that of the middle-class children. The grouping of pictures between the two socioeconomic groups revealed significant differences; nongrouping responses were significantly greater for lower-class children, showing that lower-class children have greater difficulty making groups with pictures than with the objects. Lower-class children find it easier to group three-dimensional objects in contrast to pictures. This is not true for the middle-class child (Sigel, Anderson and Shapiro, 1966; Sigel and McBane, 1967). These findings were indeed surprising in the face of the fact that the lower-class black children did have a language, a system of signs, and could use this language to label the objects. Is it not said that language, when considered a sign, is in fact representational? If this is so, how is it that these children lack representational competence?

Four other sets of data help solidify the interpretation that lower-class black children had difficulty in coping with representation in the form of the nonpresent or the inferential or re-presentation of reality.

The first is based on performance results with a group of preschool underprivileged children on the Motor Encoding Test of the Illinois Test of Psycholinguistic Abilities. It will be recalled that in this task the child is presented with a black and white picture of an object and asked to show in gestures only what is done with objects. This task is one of the most difficult ones for these underprivileged children between three and five years of age (Sigel and Perry, 1968). If the child, however, is given a three-dimensional version of the same object depicted in the picture, he has less difficulty in acting out, again in gestures, the function of the object. When given the actual object, he has no problems at all, even if unable to label it.[2]

What makes the grouping task more difficult with pictures than with three-dimensional objects? Could it be that in the three-dimensional condition the child has a wide array of cues, and perhaps more than that, he has the gestalt of the object in its spatial locale and its palpability, which are more congruent with his own

[2] These observations occurred in the course of a preschool evaluation study under the sponsorship of the Detroit Board of Education and the supervision of Mr. Burt Pryor and Dr. Donald Friedheim, Western Reserve University.

active experience with objects? Three-dimensional objects have a greater action-evocation potential than pictures. Should not pictures, as representations, however, have the same action-evocation if the picture is an acknowledged representation of the object? If the child is truly representational, the difference between the object and the picture conditions should be nonsignificant.

A second piece of evidence comes from doll-play situations with lower-class black children. The child was presented with a male adult doll, a female adult doll, and a like-sexed doll. The child was asked to tell a story using the three dolls. No other props were used. With prompting and prodding, the children provided a series of action-packed, reality-based stories; i.e., the presentation of plausible situations which appear to be reenactments of life rather than the types of condensation of symbolism so frequently associated with middle-class children. Very few importations were used. Instead, the actions attributed to the individuals were just descriptions of the acts between the objects. The lower-class child rarely used words to refer to inner feelings or inner thoughts. The stories were primarily statements of immediate actions and interactions, with little reference to the past or to the future.

A third source of evidence emerges from observation of play behavior of lower-class black children where the play of these children appears to be motoric, action-based, with animal use of imagery or pretending or role playing.

This type of play behavior is not unique to black lower-class children. Smilansky reports similar results with Israeli children who originally came from underprivileged Middle Eastern backgrounds. She found that most of the culturally disadvantaged children "do not play dramatic play at all, and those who do, play only in the especially equipped corners. Even the few plays that are organized and maintained for some time differ considerably from the average play of advantaged children" (Smilansky, 1968, p. 150).

We can now ask the question, further, is this difficulty in dealing with representations solely a function of disadvantage in a particular culture? The answer to this question will be forthcoming in a series of studies undertaken to assess the differential role of three- and two-dimensional stimuli in some types of cognitive functioning, especially memory. Second, by review of some anthropological research, it is clear that cultural differences in representational thought exist.

I would like to present some evidence to show that (a) the picture-object response discrepancy is not unique to lower-class children and (b) that this is not unique to this particular group of lower-class children. Let us first turn to a discussion of the significance of dimensionality in memory, thereby addressing ourselves to the degree to which dimensionality as a relevant variable transcends the social status of the individual. Dr. Joseph P. Jackson is involved in a series of studies at the Merrill-Palmer Institute, investigating the role of dimensionality in short- and long-term memory. He has discovered in working with seven-year-old middle-class privileged children that these children tend to be better in the recall of three-dimensional objects as compared with two-dimensional objects. Presenting a series of pairs of items, either three-dimensional or two-dimensional, he discovered that the children tended to remember the three-dimensional pairs more frequently than the two-dimensional pairs 24 hours later. This suggests then that there is a better recall with three-dimensional than two-dimensional stimuli. The explanation of this phenomenon is still moot but it does suggest that the materials are not dealt with equivalently (Jackson and Abramsky, in preparation; Sigel and Jackson, in preparation).

A number of studies done in the field of learning and/or retention with adults have found that objects tend to be more frequently recalled or more easily learned than words.

The differential responses to pictorial representation, and perhaps representation in general, vary among cultural groups — which brings us to our fourth set of evidence; namely, cultural differences in response to representations.

Hudson presents an interesting review of the major studies that have been done in South African countries. Examining the role of pictorial representation, these studies show convincingly that Bantu-speaking tribesmen had difficulty in perception of pictures as representations of three-dimensional reality. Hudson provides a vivid description of the phenomenon.

Two of the pictures, all of which were unambiguous half-tone graphic representations, produced unexpected perceptual responses in twenty protocols. One scene, representing the homecoming of a migrant industrial worker, contained the figures of an elderly couple seated in the traditional way on the ground. Behind, was a thatched round hut with the figure of a worker, clad in overalls, arms akimbo, superimposed upon it. Seven protocols referred to a winged being, a devil, an angel, the temptation of Eve in Paradise. By accident, the artist, in superimposing on the hut the foreground figure of the worker, had placed the ragged thatched roof of the hut in such a position that an observer, who perceived pictures two-dimensionally, could see the thatch as feathers or wings sprouting from the figure's back just above his shoulders. The posture with arms akimbo aided this perception (Hudson, 1967, p. 93).

Difficulties exist not only in this type of pictorial behavior but also in depth perception, where relative object size with overlapping perspective posed problems for the subjects. Just as one illustration, Hudson reports that when he presented photographs to the subjects, more than one-quarter of the Bantu pupils perceived them in two dimensions, although the pictures could be perceived in three-dimensional ways. By the end of the primary school period, the white pupils did perceive these pictures in three-dimensional perspective better than did the black pupils. In other words, *"the depth perception performance of the more highly educated black samples was not significantly better than that of the white school children of the upper class in the primary school"* (Hudson, 1967, p. 95). In effect, formal education did not significantly influence the quality of perception of two-dimensional stimuli. The implications of this difference in perspective are considerable. "Lack of understanding of the convention of perspective reduced comprehension and rendered the material of little value for teaching, and pictorial symbols capable of a literal or extended meaning tended to be interpreted literally by people of limited education" (Hudson, 1967, p. 102).

Cultural differences are not only found in regard to response to representational material in the form of pictures, but also perceptual nonrepresentational stimuli. Segall, Campbell, and Herskovitz (1966) report cultural differences in response to perceptual illusion; e.g., Muller-Lyer, etc. They claim that cultural groups vary in their susceptibility to illusions because of variable experiences in particular ecological settings.

All these studies raise the following questions:

Why is there discrepancy in object-picture classifications?

Why is there discrepancy in performance on the motor-encoding task between the three-dimensional condition and the picture condition?

Why are the storytelling and play of the disadvantaged child so heavily weighted in the direction of motoric-action level and why do they minimally contain imaginative role playing or as-if play?

Why are there cultural variations in perspective with two-dimensional stimuli?

## Representation: A Theoretical Analysis

In effect, the basic question is, "What accounts for the deficit in representational competence?"

Posing the question this way stimulated first a search of the literature for conceptualization of representation. Piaget (1962), Werner and Kaplan (1963), and Bruner (1966) are the major writers who have defined the phenomena.

For Piaget, "Representation is characterized by the fact that it goes beyond the present, extending the field of adaptation both in space and time. In other words it evokes what lies outside the immediate perceptual and active field" (Piaget, 1962, p. 273). He goes on to say, "Accordingly representation can be used in two different senses. In its broader sense representation is identical with thought, i.e., with all intelligence which is based on a system of concepts, on mental schemas, and not merely a perception of actions. In its narrower sense, representation is restricted to the mental or memory image, i.e., the symbolic evocation of absent realities" (Piaget, 1962, p. 67).

Bruner has recently offered some conceptions of representation. He has proposed three stages of representation: enactive, ikonic, and symbolic. The enactive refers to motoric behaviors; the ikonic, to imagery; and the symbolic, to language (Bruner, Olver, and Greenfield, 1966).

For Bruner, "There are two senses in which representation can be understood: in terms of the *medium* employed and in terms of its objective. With respect to the first, we can talk of three ways in which somebody 'knows' something: through doing it, through a picture or image of it, and through some such symbolic means as language. . . . understanding between the three can be achieved by viewing each as if it were external" (Bruner, Olver, and Greenfield, 1966, p. 6). The *objective* of representation for Bruner seems to be a guide to action.

Werner and Kaplan deal with the concept of representation in the context of symbols: "Correspondingly, we use the term *symbol* in two senses: in one, it is employed when we wish to emphasize a fusion or indissolubility of form and meaning; in the other, it serves to designate a pattern or configuration in some medium (sounds, lines, body movements, etc.) insofar as this pattern is taken to refer to some content" (Werner and Kaplan, 1963, p. 15). Symbols are "entities which subserve a novel and unique function, the function of *representation*. The function of representation is a constitutive mark of a symbol; it distinguishes anything qua symbol from anything qua *sign, signal,* or *thing* (Werner and Kaplan, 1963, pp. 13-14).

Representation, then, involves a reconstructing of the world of objects, thereby leading to actions guided by such representations.

Representations are distal from the world of the senses. They are not intrinsic to the object or the event, not a depiction of reality — in time, space, or content. The child has to learn that the representation is a mode of depicting instances of the physical and social world — modes which are distinct from their referent.

## The Distancing Hypothesis

Acquisition of representational competence is hypothesized as a *function* of life experiences which create temporal and/or spatial and/or psychological distance between self and object. *Distancing* is proposed as the concept to denote behaviors or events which separate the child cognitively from the immediate behavioral environment.

The behaviors or events in question are those which require the child to attend to or react in terms of the nonpresent (future/past) or the nonpalpable (abstract language). Distancing stimuli can emanate from persons or events; e.g., the mother and child discussing an anticipated birthday party or the child searching his toy chest for a particular favorite toy.

Distance is expressed in the stimuli themselves. For example, a cutout picture of a chair is closer to the chair, or less distal, than is the word "chair," simply because the latter contains no overlap of any kind with the actual reality of the chair. A photograph may be more distal than the cutout, since the cutout contains some notion of dimension or depth in its physical form, whereas the picture (photograph) only represents depth through particular visual cues. The term "distal" will be used to refer to the distance within the domain of the stimuli. Distancing refers to acts or events which may or may not employ distal stimuli to create the separation or differentiation between self and the physical environment.

In sum, then, two terms are introduced, *distal,* referring to the nature of the stimulus, and *distancing,* referring to those classes of behaviors and events which separate the person from the environment.

The distal construct is consonant with Piaget's, Bruner's, and Werner's and Kaplan's conceptualization of representational behavior. In each case there is the implicit or explicit statement that the representations of reality are separated from reality by physical or psychological *distance.* Be it the image, the picture, the symbol, or the sign, each one is distant in varying degrees from its referent.

The set of events which are hypothesized as significant determinants for the development of representation are distancing ones — where distal stimuli may or may not be employed. As we shall see, the point of view of this paper stresses the role of distancing experiences for the child, with the distal media furnishing some of the communication modalities. For example, a parent may describe in highly descriptive language an anticipated event; e.g., a trip; or a parent in preparing a child for a hospitalization experience might employ a picture book depicting hospital events *to be* experienced. These types of communications probably stimulate the child to image, to anticipate, in effect, to represent the nonpresent events.

The distance may be *temporal,* as between a past event and a present recall; *spatial,* as with a picture or image and the pictured or the imaged; in its *modality,* the name and the object; or in *degree of detail,* a sketch of an object and the object itself.

Distancing is a way to characterize differentiation of the subjective from the objective, the self from others, ideas from actions. Representational competence is hypothesized as the *resultant* of experiences creating such distance.

The technological urbanized culture in the United States is a society that employs *distancing* and requires the construction of representations to a large extent. The time emphasis, the transmission of knowledge through pictorial representation and/or graphic signs all involve representational competence.

Since these are demands of the broader cultural system as expressed in our educational system and in our middle-class environment, the difficulty found among these lower-class children becomes poignant, particularly for the Negro children. That the latter, in particular, have difficulty at the kindergarten level speaks to the possibility of continuing difficulty in school, particularly when it comes to those cognitive requirements prerequisite for academic performance.

Study of the conditions creating distance and the subsequent acquisition of representation is proposed as a research strategy in order to contribute to the remediation for those children having difficulty and also hopefully to extend our knowledge of a crucial cognitive acquisition — that of representational competence.

A search of the empirical research literature, aside from the classification studies mentioned earlier, is of little comfort. To be sure, *some* studies have demonstrated that levels of representation do in fact affect the quality of responses. Pictures elicit different responses than words in class inclusion problems (Wohlwill, 1968). Use of three-dimensional materials influence solution to conservation problems differently than verbal presentations (Sigel, Saltz, and Roskind, 1966). But on the whole, other than the work of Bruner, Piaget, and Werner and Kaplan, few detailed empirical studies are available investigating origins and functioning of representations among children.[3]

[3] There are a number of memory and learning studies among adults comparing the relative difficulty in retention of pictures vs. words or objects vs. words.

Thus, we are left with a major research task, the discovery of the conditions which define the necessary and sufficient conditions for the establishment of representational competence. In the remainder of this paper I should like to offer some specific hypotheses by which to test the distancing hypothesis.

Initially it was believed that socioeconomic differences in intellectual performance of school-age children could be attributed to differences in distancing experiences in the first two years of life. Such does not appear to be the case. Apparently environmental differences during the first two years of life are not sufficient to differentiate cognitive performance between lower- and middle-class Negro children (Golden and Birns, 1968). No socioeconomic status differences in tasks involving the displacement of objects, search for missing objects, and Cattell IQ are found. These findings suggest that at the preverbal age (before two) children from varying environments do have the ability to recall the existence of an object and to anticipate its location (Golden and Birns, 1968). Performance on such tasks indicates that rudimentary representation of the object and its place in space is present.

On the basis of these data, one is left with the conclusion that differences between lower- and middle-class children in intellectual functioning found at later ages may well have their roots in the transitionary period, the last stage of the sensorimotor intelligence and the beginning of preoperational thought, between two and four years of age approximately. It may well be that it is during this period of life that the adult assumes a more significant psychosocial role in increasing distance between self and object and hence contributes to the development of representational competence.

During this transitional period, significant experiences occur — experiences involving language and social contacts necessary for acquisition of representational thought. It is at this time in the life of the child that lower-class parents behave differently from middle-class parents in creating distance between the child and his environment.

Parents create distance in the following ways:

1. By providing a relatively orderly, structured, and sequential environment.

2. By providing a linguistic environment which contains a high frequency of words denotative of distance between referent (object) and level of language (concrete-descriptive vs. abstract-inferential).

3. By providing models indicating the relevance and pragmatic value of distancing.

Each of these conditions is hypothesized as contributing significantly to the development of representational competence because each facilitates the establishing of "distance" — spatially and temporally — between objects and their referents. The rationale for each is as follows:

1. The child *must* have an environment which is relatively orderly, structured, and sequential. The break in time-flow, the delineation of events which are nevertheless reiterated in coherent patterns, thereby structuring the world, make predictability possible not only because of the orderliness of the environment, but also because of the child's capacity for memory. These memories are particularly articulated when they serve gratification of needs. The result is the creation of a series of expectations; and what are expectations, really, but the anticipation of happenings? This anticipation is perforce represented at the preverbal level, perhaps by imagery (Decarie, 1965). In fact, there is a feedback cycle, which occurs over time, programmed as follows: an event (present), memory for it (past), and anticipation for reiteration (future). With the advent of language and stimulation to recall, evoked images are labeled and organized under particular rubrics. Language facilitates organization because particular signs can encompass a wide array of instances. The degree of stability and predictability of the environment would predict, to a high level, representational performance.

2. The content of the linguistic environment must contain a high frequency of words referring to distance in time or space and to past, present, and future to create psychological distance between reality and its reconstruction. This hypothesis refers to the types of concepts that are used in the language of adults. Lower-class children are exposed to significantly greater concrete-motoric referents and to less abstract language than middle-class children (Hess and Shipman, 1965). Language is the tool or the vehicle by which ob-

jects and events can be distanced, and the linguistic environment must provide the models.

The grammatical structure of the language must be considered. Time is expressed in tenses. But it has been reported that in the language of lower-class Negroes, time is represented grammatically in the continuous present — "I does this" — which may refer to the past, present, or future. Clear-cut delineation of the three time dimensions is apparently not made; failure to delineate may account for distancing difficulties in this group of children. Time perspective is essential in sequencing events, and ability to sequence contributes representational competence. Thus the corollary hypothesis derived from such reasoning can be stated as follows: Representational competence is negatively influenced by the lack of time-perspective concepts, those delineating distance in past and future time.

 3. The language and the orderliness of the environment can account for only some of the variance. There is still the requirement that there be opportunity for recall and reconstruction of the past and present and planning for the future. Attention by adults to the past by recalling events and stimulating discussion of what has transpired provides the child with the opportunity to imitate and participate with adults. Such experiences are hypothesized as generating imagery for the experienced past event and thereby providing the groundwork for anticipatory responses. Correct anticipatory responses reveal to the child the orderliness and, hence, predictability of the world around him.

It can be argued that these explanations place the burden of explanation on the quality and quantity of social interaction and offer very little in the way of psychological mechanisms which can be explanatory, but it must be kept in mind that the psychological mechanisms cannot be viewed in isolation from the context which stimulates them. The research on sensory deprivation highlights the significant role of particular levels and quality of response as a function of such deprivation.

I have presented in a schematic and exploratory way some ideas and hypotheses regarding the development of representational competence. Refinement of the theoretical base is still necessary, delineating levels of representations, clarifying the role of language, and spelling out in more operational terms the *distancing hypothesis*. Nevertheless, I believe the distancing hypothesis has a compelling logic that helps bring together much of the relevant theoretical literature and the few empirical studies. It helps to explain some of the data obtained with lower-class black children. The need, however, is to undertake experiments with very young black children at a preoperational level to test out these ideas. In this discussion, the problem was identified and the delineation was made of some of the variables. The challenge now is to construct significant tests of these hypotheses.

## References

Bruner, J. S., Olver, Rose R., and Greenfield, Patricia M., eds. 1966. *Studies in cognitive growth*. New York: Wiley.

Church, J. 1961. *Language and the discovery of reality: A developmental psychology of cognition*. New York: Random House.

Decarie, Therese G. 1965. *Intelligence and affectivity in early childhood: An experimental study of Jean Piaget's object concept and object relations*. Translated by Elisabeth P. Brandt and L. W. Brandt. New York: International University Press.

Golden, M., and Birns, Beverly. 1968. Social class and cognitive development in infancy. *Merrill-Palmer Quarterly* 14: 139-49.

Gollin, E. S. 1962. Factors affecting the visual recognition of incomplete objects: A comparative investigation of children and adults. *Perceptual and Motor Skills* 15: 583-90.

Hammond, K. R., ed. 1966. *The psychology of Egon Brunswik*. New York: Holt, Rinehart, and Winston.

Hess, R. D., and Shipman, Virginia C. 1965. Early experiences and the socialization of cognitive modes in children. *Child Development* 36: 869-86.

Hudson, W. 1967. The study of the problem of pictorial perception among unacculturated groups. *International Journal of Psychology* 2: 89-102.

Inhelder, Barbel, and Piaget, J. 1964. *The early growth of logic in the child: Classification and seriation*. New York: Harper and Row.

Jackson, J. P., and Abramsky, M. In preparation. The effects of dimensionality in time: A comparison of the low- and middle-class child's recognition recall.

Piaget, J. 1962. *Play, dreams, and imitation in childhood*. Translated by C. Gattegno and F. M. Hodgson. New York: Norton.

Segall, M. H., Campbell, D. T., and Herskovitz, M. J. 1966. *Influence of culture on visual perception*. Indianapolis: Bobbs-Merrill.

Sigel, I. E. 1953. Developmental trends in the abstraction ability of children. *Child Development* 24 (2): 131-44.

Sigel, I. E. 1954. The dominance of meaning. *Journal of Genetic Psychology* 85: 201-8.

Sigel, I. E., Anderson, L. M., and Shapiro, H. 1966. Categorization behavior of lower- and middle-class Negro preschool children: Differences in dealing with representation of familiar objects. *Journal of Negro Education* 35: 218-29.

Sigel, I. E., and Jackson, J. P. In preparation. The efficacy of two- vs. three-dimensionality in children's recall of familiar objects.

Sigel, I. E., and McBane, Bonnie. 1967. Cognitive competence and level of symbolization among five-year-old children. In J. Hellmuth, ed., *The disadvantaged child*, Vol. 1. Seattle, Washington: Special Child Publications, pp. 435-53.

Sigel, I. E., and Olmsted, Patricia P. 1969. Modification of classificatory competence and level of representation among lower-class Negro kindergarten children. Final Report, Head Start, 1966-67. In A. H. Passow, ed., *Reaching the disadvantaged learner*. New York: Columbia University, Teachers College Press.

Sigel, I. E., and Perry, Cereta. 1968. Psycholinguistic diversity among "culturally deprived" children. *American Journal of Orthopsychiatry* 38: 122-26.

Sigel, I. E., Saltz, E., and Roskind, W. 1966. Variables determining concept conservation in children. *Journal of Experimental Psychology* 4: 471-75.

Smilansky, S. 1968. *The effects of socio-dramatic play on disadvantaged preschool children*. New York: Wiley.

Werner, H., and Kaplan, E. 1963. *Symbol formation; an organismic-developmental approach to language and expression of thought*. New York: Wiley.

Wohlwill, J. 1968. Responses to class-inclusion questions for verbally and pictorially presented items. *Child Development* 39: 449-66.

# PART II

## Training Procedures

# 4

GENEVIEVE PAINTER

# A Tutorial Language Program
# for Disadvantaged Infants

## I. The Case for Infant Training

It is generally agreed that children of the poor are not adequately prepared to achieve their respectful place in society. This is not only a social loss, but a personal loss as well. Where the difficulty lies, no one is quite sure. A study of infant development (birth to 16 months) revealed no differences along socioeconomic lines; however, developmental deficits are well established in children from culturally disadvantaged families by the age of three (Bayley, 1965; Pasamanick and Knoblock, 1961). We do not know the best time for intervening in the developmental process, for we do not know precisely which years are critical for later development. However, research suggests that the earlier intervention begins, the greater are the gains which occur (Bloom, 1964; Kirk, 1964). The question of whether or not preschool experience can help to compensate for developmental deficits is no longer seriously debated; the controversy now focuses on the defenders of the traditional or child-centered nursery school program and the proponents of a structured preschool curriculum. Reports to date of research projects involving curriculum innovation seem to indicate that a partially structured curriculum, as compared with the completely unstructured, is more likely to effect significant changes in the development of disadvantaged preschool children and infants (Weikart, 1967; Karnes et al., 1966; Painter, 1967, 1968).

Bloom, in reviewing the effects of variations in environment on intelligence, estimated that 50 percent of intellectual development takes place "between conception and age 4, about 30 percent between ages 4 and 8, and about 20 percent between ages 8 and 17" (1964, p. 88). Other investigators support Bloom and suggest that children of deprived environments can make greater cognitive gains when intervention begins early in life. In a study by Skeels and Dye (1939), 13 mentally retarded children ages 7.1 to 35.9 months were transferred from an orphanage to institutional wards for older, high-grade, mentally defective girls who gave the infants extensive care, attention, and affection. The control group of similar age and intelligence remained at the orphanage and received no special attention. The experimental group showed a mean IQ increase of 27.5 points; the control subjects showed a mean loss of 26.2 IQ points. Skeels (1964) followed up the experimental and control children 21 years later. Eleven of the 13 experimental children had been placed in adoptive homes in childhood. All were self-supporting and none a ward of an institution; their median grade completed in school was twelfth grade. Of the 12 control children who had remained in the orphanage for a prolonged period, one-half were wards of institutions. The median grade they completed was third grade.

Kirk (1958) reported on two groups of mentally retarded children being raised in an institution. One group of 15, with a mean age of four and one-half years, was given preschool education each day. The mean increase in their IQ scores was over ten points. Six of the experimental children were later paroled from the institution, while a contrast group of similar age and mental ability was left in the wards. The latter group showed a mean decrease of six IQ points.

Kirk (1962) later compared two groups of mentally retarded children living in the community. The experimental group was given preschool education. Followup studies after age six showed that those who had the advantage of foster-home placement in addition to preschool training made the greatest mental and social growth. Children brought up in their own inadequate homes and given only preschool class improved, but to a lesser extent. Those who had neither a change of environment nor preschool changed for the worse when they changed at all.

Other studies show that when retardates enter school at six years of age, although school environment is more stimulating than home environment, the increase in IQ is only six or seven points (Kirk, 1958; Goldstein, Moss, and Jordan, 1964; Smith and Stroud, 1960). The studies also reveal that retardates who receive stimulation which begins during ages one to three differ from contrast groups by over 50 IQ points. When stimulation is introduced at ages four and five, the increase in IQ is less than one-half of that produced by stimulation at an earlier age. And when intervention begins as a result of school entry at age six, the increase in IQ is only half the increment accruing when the child begins preschool two years earlier (Kirk, 1964).

It seems obvious that the emphasis should be on the prevention of educational deficits rather than compensation for deficits which inadvertently develop. Therefore, interest in the education of infants is now increasing at a phenomenal rate. Research and service organizations are attempting to educate infants in their homes, in community centers, and in day care centers; these organizations are also teaching groups of mothers to educate their own infants. School systems are beginning to take responsibility for education at all levels and some are developing programs which include teaching parents methods of child training, as well as preschool programs for children from birth to four years. Working cooperatively in this effort are public health nurses, social workers, other helping professionals, and nonprofessional mothers trained as study-group discussion leaders.

The U.S. Office of Economic Opportunity has funded 36 parent-child centers for low-income families in various parts of the country. These centers offer educational services to parents and their children from birth to three years. Several of these centers have infants as young as six months in daily, two-hour "school" programs. Many centers are using the educational play activities described in this paper and are training mothers to assist the professional teachers in the classrooms. Mothers are also being trained to lead other mothers in study-group discussions on child-rearing practices.[1]

## II. An Overview of the Tutorial Language Program

Much has been written describing the spontaneous intellectual growth of infants (Gesell, 1940; Piaget, 1963), but little can be found concerning either theory or practice of planned acceleration of development. In answer to the question "What shall we teach?" this paper presents a rationale for and description of infant language training, including specific suggestions for that training. It is the belief of the writer that these suggestions can be used by professional teachers, paraprofessionals after some training, and parents. The instructions in this paper are directed toward the teacher. An adaptation has been made for parents who serve as teachers.[2]

Included in the program is training for conceptual development, because culturally disadvantaged children have generally been found to perform at a lower level than their advantaged peers in both areas. However, the differentiation between language growth and conceptual growth in an individual is only theoretical, since they actually proceed together in the spontaneous development of the child. They are presented independently of each other in this paper for purposes of structuring the program.

Culturally disadvantaged infants are not usually deficient in motor development. However, infants learn through sensory input, and motor skills are developing during the first year of life. Sensory-motor training can be used to facilitate the development of concepts and language. Visual, auditory, tactual, kinesthetic, olfactory, and gustatory modalities should be stressed independently and in combinations in the various activities. Infants should be encouraged to give both verbal and motor responses. An appropriate age for initiation of this phase of intervention is between 10 and 12 months; earlier

[1] The text which is read and discussed in these mothers' study groups is *Children: the Challenge* by Rudolf Dreikurs, and Vicki Soltz (New York: Meredith Press, 1964). This book offers a simple, practical application of a theoretically based philosophy of democratic child rearing which is applicable to middle-class as well as low-income families.

[2] Genevieve Painter, *Teach Your Baby* (New York: Simon and Schuster, 1970).

training is not proposed here because language development is not sufficiently advanced.

The training procedures to be described here were developed in connection with a research project[3] that was part of a larger project designed to determine the strategic age at which environmental intervention will produce maximum acceleration of cognitive development in culturally disadvantaged children.[4] The initial phase of the study of infants had two major purposes: (a) the development of a tutorial program for infants in their homes and (b) the evaluation of the infants' progress after a one-year period of tutoring.

Twenty Negro and Caucasian infants, male and female, who were siblings of four-year-olds attending an experimental nursery school for the disadvantaged, composed the sample. They ranged in age between 8 and 24 months; medical examination revealed no evidence of physical limitation, and measured intelligence was within the range of 80 to 120 on the Cattell Infant Intelligence Scale (Cattell, 1960). They were randomly assigned to experimental and control groups.

Female tutors worked individually with each experimental subject in his home for one hour a day, five days a week, over a period of one year. The tutors had varying professional backgrounds — in music, child development, nursing, and elementary education. They were selected on the basis of their experience and interest in working with young children. An orientation week initiated tutor training.

An assessment of each experimental subject was made to determine his level of development, content of the program, and teaching procedures. In general, the assessment suggested that training should emphasize language development, symbolic representation, and concept formation. Each child was given a program designed to ameli-

[3] The complete research report is contained in Genevieve Painter, *The Effect of a Tutorial Program on the Intellectual Development of Disadvantaged Infants* (1967, available on microfilm from Dissertation Abstracts, Ann Arbor, Mich.) and *Infant Education* (San Rafael, Calif.: Dimensions Publishing Co., 1968). Included in both volumes are assessment procedures, full reviews of the literature, the rationale of the training program, logistics of tutoring in the home, and complete analysis of data, as well as the training program which is presented in this paper with modifications.

[4] Merle B. Karnes, Research Project on the Disadvantaged, supported by a grant from the Bureau of Research, U.S. Office of Education (USOE5-1181, Contract 6-10-235).

orate the developmental lags found in the initial assessment. The program was changed in the course of treatment to take account of progress. During weekly home visits, the writer (who served as program supervisor), together with the child's tutor, observed the child's performance and evaluated the effectiveness of the training. The child's progress was then compared periodically with developmental schedules. Inservice training of tutors continued on a weekly basis throughout the year. The supervisor met individually with tutors and conducted group training sessions. At these sessions the activities were evaluated for their appropriateness to a given child's progress and for their general interest to children of this age.

The first three or four weeks of the training were spent in non-structured activities to establish rapport and to study the child's development. During this time gross motor play with balls, wagons, and pull toys was initiated, as well as small-muscle activities with beads and puzzles. Gross motor play was decreased as the structured program was initiated, and the child was then required to sit at a table and work for longer periods of time. A Baby Tenda (a square table about 18 inches high, with a canvas seat in the middle) was used for the younger children; either a child-sized table and chair or a junior chair at a kitchen table was used for older children.

As many as 13 tasks were given the child in a single session to maintain his interest while working. His attention span was gradually increased by extending the length of time on an individual activity. After the child became accustomed to working at length at a single activity, then the number of activities was again increased so that more types of tasks could be mastered. Each child was trained to sit and work at his table for a full hour at each session; he was able to work without frustration for this period of time because he experienced satisfaction in his work. At no time were extrinsic rewards given to a child. Encouragement and intrinsic motivation (satisfaction in his own accomplishment) were the only reinforcers used.

## III. Educational Program

### A. Language Training

It is generally agreed that an infant utters his first word when he is about one year old. However, he is actually learning about *how* to speak from the moment of the birth cry. For the first weeks his crying is undifferentiated except that he may cry louder or softer at times. Soon the mother is able to tell if the child is crying because of hunger or because of discomfort due to the need of a diaper change. The infant is learning about the use of his vocal mechanism by feeling the air flow in and out of his throat, nose, and mouth by sucking, swallowing, belching, and gurgling. Perhaps most important of all, he is learning that vocal activity can be useful in communicating wants and needs.

The infant understands what is said to him long before he is able to talk. He understands by the attending adult's actions and from the situation in which an event occurs. If the infant were told only, "Open your mouth," he probably would not understand. However, if his mother says "Open your mouth" while she has a spoon in her hand and she is feeding him, he probably begins to understand what he is expected to do.

An outline of training procedures follows. The time for instruction of a particular type of training is included, but is, of course, only an approximation.

### 1. Initiation of training: imitation of the actions of others (10 months).

During the first year of life, the infant engages in many imitative activities which are related to language development. When his mother smiles, he smiles in return. When he coos, his mother makes his sounds. He will learn to imitate the sounds of others, but he will first be able to imitate the actions of others. The following activities are suggested for teaching the infant to imitate movement; the teacher should do the movement and the child will soon learn to imitate.

Move your head from side to side.

Wave and say "bye-bye."

Play "bouncy-bouncy." Bounce the infant up and down as you sit holding him on your lap. He will try to continue the movement even when you stop. (According to Piaget, he is learning how to make an interesting experience last.)

Hit the table with your hand.

Wave a toy in the air.

Hit a toy with a stick.

Pretend to drink from a toy cup; give him the cup.

Hold a block in each hand and hit them together.

Pat your hands together as in "pat-a-cake."

While the child is sitting on your lap, facing you, put your forehead against his and say "boom." Take your head away and do it again. The infant will learn to move his head toward yours.

Play with toys and let him imitate your movement.

## 2. Training the infant to imitate sounds (12 months).

The following imitative activities are suggested for teaching the infant to repeat sounds. Initiate these when the infant is babbling at you.

Say a sound that he has already said himself and laugh as you say it. If he repeats the sound, you repeat it, too, thus playing a game.

Choose a simple sound which you have not heard him say before. Laugh and see if he will say the new sound; if he does say it, repeat.

Smack your lips as in kissing.

Whistle and see if he will pucker up his lips and try to whistle.

Make a coughing sound.

Breath hard and make a panting sound.

Say "burr," "aboo," "oh, oh," "grrr."

Put your finger over your mouth and say "sh."

Put your hand over your mouth, Indian style, and say "wah, wah, wah."

Play "This Little Piggy Went to Market." Let him have a turn to say "wee, wee, wee."

Use the words and sounds that go naturally with an activity, "wee," "zoom," "boom," "wow," "oh, oh," "all gone."

## 3. Training in identifying and naming objects (14 months).

Show the infant objects found in the home and tell him their names. If he is unable to say the words, encourage him to point to the object or to go and get it. "Where is the cup?" "Get your shoe." When he is able to name objects, encourage him to say the names. While you point to a bar of soap say, "What is this? Yes, soap."

### 4. Teaching the child to verbalize needs and wants (16 months).

When the child points to an item which he wants, tell him how to ask for it. If he is only able to say a single word and not pronounce it perfectly, accept his effort at first. For example, if he wants water but only points to the sink and grunts, tell him, "water." He may only be able to say "wah-wah" at first. When his speech becomes more precise, say "wa-ter" very distinctly and try to solicit the word from him. Model "I want water" and reinforce his use of the sentence with praise and warmth.

Show him an object and a picture of the object cut from a magazine. Paste the picture on a paper sack so that he can carry through on an action. Say, "Orange. Put the orange with its picture" or "Put the orange in its bag." Any object and its picture may be used (comb, spoon, cup, toothbrush). Give him *one* object and *two* pictures from which to choose — an orange and pictures of an orange and of a banana. Say, "Put the orange with its picture." Show him two pictures and ask him to point to one and then to the other. Say, "Show me the apple" and "Now, show me the orange."

Give him two objects and two pictures and say, "Put the orange with its picture, and put the toothbrush with its picture" (or "in its bag"). Do the same with three pictures and three objects and, finally, with four pictures and three objects (three pictures matching objects and the fourth picture not matching).

Show him pictures in books and tell him their names. Then ask him, "What is this?" or "What do you call this?"

Start a scrapbook for him. Cut pictures from magazines and help him paste them into the book. If he cannot say the names of the pictures, give him two at a time; and while naming one, have him point to it. Say, "Show me the dog." If he points to the dog, give it to him to paste into the book. Later on, when he is able to say words, give him the picture to paste only when he actually says the name; say, "This is a cat. What is this?" "Yes, a cat. Good. You may have the picture for your book." He will take great pride in his very own book and will react with pleasure to its use in subsequent lessons.

## 5. Introducing picture books (18 to 24 months).

After he is able to work with individual pictures, show him picture books. The first books should be simple and uncluttered, with a story involving only one major object; for example, *The Apple Book* or *The Elephant Book*. Talk only about the pictures and do not tell an involved story at first. Try to have him name the things he sees. When he gets older and understands more speech, read him simple stories from books.

## 6. Teaching the child to use elaborative language (18 months).

Extend the child's speech and encourage spontaneous speech in dramatic play, rhymes, songs, and other activities.

Use puppets with the child in telling stories and in acting out the stories.

Use a toy telephone to encourage speech.

Show him action pictures of children or adults (a woman sweeping, a child throwing a ball or gardening). Ask him, "What is the boy doing?" Tell him if he does not know, and then ask him again.

Teach him adverbs and adjectives by using them yourself and encouraging him to repeat your statement. "This car goes *fast.*" "This is a *red* block."

Teach him the use of prepositions by using objects, parts of the body, and paper dolls. "Put the penny *in* the box, *on* the chair, *between* your toes." "Put the father *in front of* the mother, *in back of* the sister, *beside* the brother, *between* the mother and sister."

The following antonyms may be taught through simple play activities or through pictures.

*Boy-Girl:* brother, sister, pictures of children.

*Cry-Laugh:* dramatic play, looking in a mirror.

*Up-Down:* throwing the ball up and watching it fall down, playing "Ring Around the Rosey" (all fall *down*).

*Full-Empty:* filling glass with juice (full), drinking it (then it's empty).

*Hard-Soft:* touching sponge, stone, feather, cotton, wood.

*Big-Little:* cars, boxes, balls.

*Open-Shut:* (or *Open-Close*): book, box, pictures of items opened and closed.

*Quiet-Loud:* rhythm instruments, radio.
*Slow-Fast:* walking, running, playing with cars.

### 7. Encouraging internal dialogue (24 months).

Problem solving is simplified when under the control of internalized language. The individual carries on an internal dialogue which differs from the speech he uses in communication. Teach the child to plan with words as he solves a problem. For example, when he is putting together a puzzle, you can say, "We start with the head; turn it around slowly until the piece will fit; put it in." Have the child say it with you as he completes the puzzle. After he learns to say it aloud, tell him to whisper it. And still later tell him to say it to himself.

### B. Concept Training

Concepts of body image, space, number, time, and classification were selected for emphasis in this training program because they are believed to be necessary prerequisites for academic learning and can be understood by children at an early age if appropriately presented.

### 1. Body image (14 months).

Body image is the mental picture one has of his own body and its parts at a given moment in time. The following activities may be used to help the child develop a clear and concise concept of body image.

Ask the child to point to his eye, nose, ear, etc. while looking into a mirror.

Ask the child to show you your eye and compare his eye as seen in a mirror.

Include other body parts in the same manner. Ask him to name parts of the body when he is able to talk.

Point to his eye and ask, "What is this?"

Let him eat fruit or a cookie while observing himself in the mirror.

Verbalize the words "tongue," "mouth," "teeth," and "chewing."

Tell the child to imitate your movement while looking in a mirror.

Blink your eyes, wave your hand, move your head.

Show him a doll or puppet and tell him to name the parts of the body.

Ask him to name parts of the body of people or animals while looking at pictures in a book. Ask, "Where is the dog's eye?"

Have him place his hand or foot on paper and draw an outline.

Let him color the picture.

Allow the child to lie down on a large piece of shelf paper. Trace an outline of his body with a magic marker. Put the picture on a wall with tape and have the child color the picture to match the colors of his clothing.

Draw a circle and ask the child to place eyes, nose, and mouth on the "face."

Draw a picture of a human figure with a distortion (arms coming from head instead of shoulders, mouth missing) and ask, "What is wrong with this picture?"

Make a doll of felt pieces and have the child put the doll together on a felt board.

Sing action songs and have the child do the actions with you ("I Am Very Small, I Am Very Tall," "Put Your Finger on Your Nose, On Your Nose," "If You're Happy and You Know It, Clap Your Hands").

While lying on the floor, show the child how to stretch and relax to feel the muscles contract and relax.

While lying on the floor, have the child move both legs, both arms, one leg, one arm, left leg and left arm, left leg and right arm. He should keep arms and legs in contact with floor as he moves. Let him pretend that he is your mirror; he can imitate your movements (touch head, elbow, knee; blink eye; put out tongue). Reverse roles; imitate his movements and become the child's mirror.

### 2. Space (10 months).

The infant is learning about things in space, about himself in space, and about space itself. The following activities will help this learning.

Put a toy close to him so that he can reach it easily. Then put the toy farther from him so that he has to reach with more effort.

Place two blocks on the table out of easy reach, one to his right and one to his left. He will learn to reach to either side of himself.

While holding him, put his bottle or toy on the table. Turn yourself and him away from it so that your back is toward the table. See if he will turn himself around to see it.

While both of you are sitting on the floor facing each other, shake a small toy until his eyes are on it. Move it along the floor slowly until you push it behind your own back. See if he will crawl around you to find it.

Now move the toy along the floor until it is directly behind *him*. See if he will turn his body around to see the toy.

Arrange furniture so that he can creep through narrow and low spaces (between chairs, between couch and wall, under a low table). He will learn how he relates to a given amount of space.

Place him near a staircase and place a toy on the second step. In climbing to get the toy, he will learn about up and down and about depth, too.

Show him a picture upside down that he knows well. See if he will turn his head to see the picture upright. Turn the picture upright and then try the whole activity again.

Raise and lower him while you say "up, down"; he will enjoy this game and will learn the feeling of up and down.

Give him doughnut blocks to play with so that he will see and feel that there is an inside and an outside. Then give him a spindle upon which he may place the blocks.

Show him a stuffed animal with its face toward him. When he starts to reach for it, quickly turn it around so that he sees the back of the animal. When he takes it in his hand, watch him to see if he will turn it around to see the face again.

Put some small toys inside a cup and hand them to him. He will probably take them out one at a time and then put them back into the cup. Show him that he can turn the whole cup over and make the toys fall out all at once. Give him the toys in the cup again and see if he will then turn the entire cup over to get the toys out.

### (a) More activities involving space (16 months).

Show him how to hang clothes on hooks and towels on rods. He will learn about up and down as well as learning how to hang things.

Give him a form box in which he can place cylinders in round holes and cubes in square holes, etc. Start with the cylinders; they will be the easiest to place. As he learns the task, add the other forms gradually. (Several toy companies make a box with five shapes: cylinder, cube, square, triangle, and arch. Be sure that you select a well-made toy for this activity; those made of wood are made with more precision and seem to be easier to place than those of plastic.)

**(b) Introduce jigsaw juzzles.**

Start with three-piece puzzles and then add those which are more complicated.

Geometric shapes can be taught in freehand drawing with finger paints, watercolors, crayons, and magic markers with which you and the child can make circles, squares, and triangles.

Use templates to trace circles, squares, and triangles.

Size can be easily taught by placing graduated rings upon a pyramid-shaped structure, the largest fitting on the bottom and the smallest on top. Start with only three rings at first, and when the child learns to place these properly, give him additional rings for placement. Pieces of cardboard can be used for matching, identifying, and naming sizes — big, little, middle-sized.

**(c) Introduce matching activities.**

Cut two circles out of grey or white cardboard, one twice the size of the other, and place them on his table. Cut two more like the others and give him one in his hand and say, "Put this one with the one just like it." Or give him both and say, "Put the big one with the big one and the little one with the little one." (All should be the same color, so that you do not confuse teaching color with teaching size.)

Place one large and one small cardboard on the table and say, "Give me the big one" and "Give me the little one."

Point to one of the cardboard circles and say, "Which one is this, the big one or the little one?" Later, use three sizes presented in the same manner: big, little, and middle-sized.

**(d) Introduce seriation.**

Place nested cups or boxes in order. Start with only three cups which fit into each other easily; then add more.

## (e) Teach the child to copy designs.

Three or four poker chips or buttons can be placed on a sheet of paper in various relationships to each other, making designs. Give the child an equal number of chips or buttons and a sheet of paper and ask him to copy your design.

The same idea can be used with pegboards, but start with simple designs.

## 3. Teaching number concepts.

The child can start learning about numbers when quite young (about 14 months). Here are suggestions for activities.

Place pennies or bits of cereal on his table. Ask him for "one."

Show him "one," if he doesn't respond. Then ask him for "more," or "many."

Play "one for me and one for you." Place two cups on the table, one in front of the child and the other in front of yourself. Tell the child to put one piece of cereal or a penny in his cup and then one in your cup until all the pennies or cereal bits are placed.

Give him two boxes and tell him to put one penny in each. Then show him how many are "two" and tell him to hold "two" in his fingers and then put two in each box. (He will not understand that "one" and then "one" more are "two" at first; he will see "two" only when they make a unit of two.) Since this task is difficult, it may be necessary to make up a story or game to play; such as, "Give Mother two pennies in her box; then give yourself two pennies in your box. Now, we'll go to the store and buy candy for you and Mother." Move the boxes to another corner of the table, and let him pretend to give the pennies to the storekeeper.

Teach the child to count by rote from one to five and later to ten. He will, of course, not know the meaning of the words, but he will understand that these are words used in counting.

Show him how to count the fingers on each hand.

Use counting songs and books with counting games.

Have the child count cookies or pieces of candy before eating them.

Teach the child to count blocks as he stacks them.

Cut numerals from cardboard or sandpaper and tell him their names.

## 4. Time.

Without a sense of the passage of time, a child will not be able to learn to "be on time" when he reaches school age. However, it is difficult to teach the concept of time. Even adults have difficulty with the concept.

Typically a child learns about time as he experiences an orderly sequence of events in a well-run home. He hears, "Time to get up," "Time for breakfast," "Time for play," "Time for nap," and "Time for Daddy to come home." As each day goes along similarly to the last one, he begins to *feel* a sense of the passage of time and of the order of daily events. The following suggestions may be used to teach the child about time.

Use the words "after" and "before" so that he can learn about the past, present, and future. "*After* you drink your milk, you may have the cookie." "You must take a nap *before* we go outdoors." "*Now* you can go outside."

Use the appropriate vocabulary to express time. When he wants something and you are busy, say, "Just a minute" or "In a moment." He will learn that these words mean a short delay.

Relate events to the time of their occurrence: "Time to eat," "Time to go home," "It is 10 o'clock and time for juice."

Use the words "yesterday," "today," and "tomorrow." "*Yesterday* was a rainy day; *today* is a sunny day."

Use different tenses in talking to the child: "I *did* it yesterday," "We *went*," "We'll do it."

Use comparative adjectives to indicate differences in amount of time needed for an activity: "slower," "faster."

## 5. Classification.

The child learns to understand his world better when he learns to put things into categories. The following activities are suggested to help the child learn about classification.

*Color* can be taught by first matching colors. Put a red sock on the child's foot and then show him one red and one blue sock and say, "Which one goes with the one on your foot?" You can try this activity before the child talks because it does not require speech. Use the three primary colors, red, blue, and yellow; allow him to choose from two colors to match the one on his foot.

Allow him to choose from three colors after he is successful with the above.

Place the sock on the foot of a doll and have the child match the color on the doll's foot.

Matching, identifying, and naming colors can be taught with colored cardboard chips.

*Matching:* Place two colored chips on the table (either red and blue, red and yellow, or blue and yellow). Give the child one of the colors and say, "Put this one with the one just like it." After he learns to choose from two colors, use three.

*Identifying:* Put two colors on the table and say, "Give me the red one" and "Now give me the yellow one." This may take time to teach. It is much easier to match than to select the right one by name. Later, let the child choose from three colors.

*Naming:* Place the colors on the table and say, "What color is this one?"

*Extend color lessons to the environment:* Tell the child to point to or name colors of objects found in the home.

*Sameness and Difference* can be taught with pictures. Place two pictures on the table and ask the child to find one that is the *same* as the one in your hand. Then let him choose from three and then four pictures. Place three or four pictures, all alike but one, on the table and say, "Give me the one that is *not* like the others." (*"Not like"* is easier to understand than "different"; later use the word "different.")

*Picture Classification* can be taught by cutting out pictures from popular magazines. Very young children can sort people, dogs, cats, birds, foods, and other pictures. Paste a picture of a dog on the bottom of an opened box and a picture of a bird on another box. Give the child pictures of five dogs and five birds and say, "Put the dogs in the dog house and the birds in the birds' nest." (It is easier to give the child one picture at a time at first.) After he can sort five pictures of two categories, try 10 and then 15 pictures in each category. Change the categories for variety. Later increase the number of categories.

## IV. Evaluation of the Infant Training Program

On the initial testing when the program was inaugurated, the infants were found to be average in intelligence and in motoric development but below their chronological age in language development, in interpretation of symbolic representation, and in conceptual development. The tutorial program described above was designed to ameliorate these deficits.

| Variable | IQ | |
| --- | --- | --- |
| | Experimental Group | Control Group |
| Cattell (pretest) | | |
| Mean Month CA | 15.5 | 15.7 |
| Mean Month MA | 15.3 | 15.2 |
| Mean IQ | 98.8 | 98.4 |
| Binet (posttest) | | |
| Mean Month CA | 29.2 | 29.0 |
| Mean Month MA | 32.7 | 29.2 |
| Mean IQ | 108.1 | 98.8 |

Note: Motor, language, and representation were assessed with Fokes, Gesell — no formal scores available — concepts on Hunt-Uzgiris (experimental edition).

A summary of posttest data follows:

1. Although the groups were found to be comparable on pretest measures, the experimental group mean IQ on the Stanford-Binet at the posttest was 108.1 and that of the control group was 98.8, significant at the .05 level.
2. On postlanguage development tests — Illinois Test of Psycholinguistic Abilities (ITPA) and the language subtests of the Merrill-Palmer Scale of Mental Tests — the sample values of the experimental group were superior on all but one ITPA subtest. The .05 level of significance was reached on two subtests.

3. On all eight tests administered to assess conceptual development, the sample values of the experimental group were found to be consistently superior to those of the control group. Five of these tests differed at the .05 level of significance.

4. Seven tests were used to assess sensory-motor development. On all but one test the sample values of the experimental group only slightly exceeded those of the control group, thus confirming our assumption that culturally disadvantaged children are not deficient in motoric development. Statistically significant differences were found on only one of these tests.

## V. Some Recommendations

Although much has been written in the field of child development describing the spontaneous intellectual growth of infants, little is to be found concerning either efforts or theories relative to consciously sought and planned acceleration of language and cognitive growth. In view of the lack of previous studies of this latter nature and the lack of a comprehensive theory related to children at this level, it was necessary for this training program to utilize an almost completely eclectic approach with ideas drawn from child development theory, common sense, trial and error, and even, in some cases, intuition. When we had doubts about any practices and procedures, they were dropped and replaced by activities suggested by the tutors and the writer, who served as program supervisor. It is hoped that the activities, materials, and procedures described in this paper may serve as guidelines for people who plan to work in the field of infant education.

The results of our study, although involving only 20 infants, strongly suggest that the activities and content of the tutorial program produced within the experimental group a rate of acceleration substantially greater than that of the control group. Extensions of the study, other than by replication or elaboration, might move in two or three directions. In the present study, little was done to involve mothers in the tutoring program. The primary purpose of the study was the development of a curriculum to be administered and assessed by professional teachers. One possible extension would be the organization of a program of instruction for mothers so that their child-rearing practices and daily conduct of the household would contribute to the intellectual growth of the child. One such research extension (Badger, 1969) is reported to have been very effective. The mothers, who attended weekly group meetings where they learned an infant-education approach, teaching methods, and improved child-rearing practices, were most enthusiastic. They applied the program at home in daily lessons and their infants have made educational gains.

Services to lower socioeconomic families are presently found in Parent-Child Centers established by the U.S. Office of Economic Opportunity and in other agencies. They now include programs of infant tutoring by outsiders and programs in which mothers are taught to teach their own infants. A third possibility exists for infant education in day care centers. Most day care centers do not admit children under the age of two and one-half, but some are now beginning to realize the advisability of expanding their services to include infants. Center personnel are also becoming aware of the need to take responsibility for stimulating and educating infants and young children, rather than giving infants mere custodial care. The procedures developed in this study may provide guidelines for inaugurating new services and extending old ones to include infant education.

An ultimate extension of our infant study would involve the actual extension of the public school system into a subnursery program offering services to the entire community. The problems of logistics and high cost in home tutoring point to the desirability of having infants attend a central instructional facility where organized care and propitiously structured living routines would free the program of many typical problems existing in the disadvantaged home. The structured-play activities described here can be carried on with several infants at a time. Infants attending such centers could be provided with opportunities for intellectual stimulation, constructive play, and socialization, as well as the necessary rest, nourishment, and warmth we have long associated with sound infant care.

## References

Badger, Earladeen. 1969. Mothers' training program: Educational intervention by the mothers of disadvantaged infants. Mimeographed. Urbana, Ill.: Institute for Research on Exceptional Children, University of Illinois.

Bayley, Nancy. 1965. Comparison of mental and motor test scores for ages 1-15 months by sex, birth order, race, geographical location and education of parents. *Child Development* 36: 379-411.

Bereiter, C., and Engelmann, S. 1966. *Teaching disadvantaged children in the preschool.* Englewood Cliffs, N.J.: Prentice-Hall.

Bloom, B. S. 1964. *Stability and change in human characteristics.* New York: Wiley.

Cattell, Psyche. 1960. *The measurement of the intelligence of infants and young children.* New York: Psychological Corp.

Dreikurs, R. 1968. *Psychology in the classroom.* New York: Harper and Row.

Dreikurs, R., and Soltz, Vicki. 1964. *Children: The challenge.* New York: Meredith.

Gesell, A., et al. 1940. *The first five years of life: A guide to the study of the preschool child.* New York: Harper.

Goldstein, H., Moss, J. W., and Jordan, Laura J. 1964. The efficacy of special class training on the development of mentally retarded children. Mimeographed. Urbana, Ill.: Institute for Research on Exceptional Children, University of Illinois.

Karnes, Merle B., et al. 1966. *A comparative study of two preschool programs for culturally disadvantaged children: A highly structured and traditional program.* Urbana, Ill.: Institute for Research on Exceptional Children, University of Illinois.

Kirk, S. A. 1958. *Early education of the mentally retarded.* Urbana, Ill.: University of Illinois Press.

Kirk, S. A. 1962. Effects of educational treatment. *Mental Retardation,* Research publication of Association for Research in Nervous and Mental Disease 39: 289-94.

Kirk, S. A. 1964. The challenge of individual differences. In Melvin M. Tumin and Marvin Bressler, eds., *Proceedings of a conference on quality and equality in education.* Princeton University. Princeton, N.J.: Princeton University Press.

Kirk, S. A., McCarthy, J. J., and Kirk, Winifred. 1968. *The Illinois Test of Psycholinguistic Abilities.* Revised ed. Urbana, Ill.: University of Illinois Press.

*Merrill-Palmer Scale of Mental Tests.* 1948. New York: Harcourt, Brace and World.

Painter, Genevieve. 1967. The effect of a tutorial program on the intellectual development of disadvantaged infants. Doctoral dissertation, University of Illinois.

Painter, Genevieve. 1968. *Infant education.* San Rafael, Calif.: Dimensions.

Painter, Genevieve. 1970. *Teach your baby.* New York: Simon and Schuster.

Pasamanick, B., and Knoblock, H. 1961. Epidemiologic studies on the complications of pregnancy and the birth process. In C. Caplan, ed., *Prevention of mental disorders in children*. New York: Basic Books, pp. 74-94.

Piaget, J. 1963. *The origins of intelligence in children*. New York: Norton.

Skeels, H. M. 1964. An interim brief on the NIMH-Iowa follow-up studies relative to mental retardation, dependency and maternal deprivation. Mimeographed. Bethesda, Md.: National Institute of Mental Health.

Skeels, H. M., and Dye, H. B. 1939. A study of the effects of differential stimulation on mentally retarded children. *Procedures of American Association on Mental Deficiency* 44: 114-36.

Smith, L. L., and Stroud, J. B. 1960. Effects of a comprehensive opportunity program on the development of educable mentally retarded children. Mimeographed. Iowa City: State University of Iowa.

*Stanford-Binet Intelligence Scale, Form L-M (Revised)*. 1960. Boston: Houghton Mifflin.

Weikart, D. 1967. Preschool programs: Preliminary findings. *Journal of Special Education* 1: 163-81.

# 5

CELIA STENDLER LAVATELLI, EDITOR[1]

# A Systematized Approach to Language Teaching: The Tucson Method

A unique and promising model for compensatory education has been developed in the primary grades of the Tucson, Arizona, public schools, under the direction of Dr. Marie Hughes. Special features of the model, relevant for language training, are described in this paper; a complete report is being prepared by Dr. Hughes.

The children in the program are Spanish-American six-, seven-, and eight-year-olds. It had been the custom of the public school to assign these children to special classes at school entrance, because they knew so little English. One-third of the children in such classes typically were not ready for first grade after a year but had to continue in the same class for an additional year.

In initiating the project, researchers noted that in these special classes there were infrequent opportunities for language practice. The teacher did most of the talking; individual children rarely uttered a sentence. When the teacher asked a question, the children answered in a chorus. The school program provided little opportunity for using language to express ideas. In addition, it was noted that the children gave evidence of being afraid to participate in the school program; in fact, most teachers cited "shyness" as one of the factors entering into nonpromotion.

The first language tests given to the children before the experimental program was begun showed that the children who knew the

---

[1] Prepared by Celia B. Lavatelli from materials supplied by Dr. Hughes and Mrs. Arline Hobson.

most English also knew the most Spanish, while the children who knew the least English were also poor in Spanish. Therefore it was decided to use English as the language of instruction since the Spanish of the children who needed the program most was inadequate to the task. While it was recognized that there is a psychological danger in selecting English — the language of the ethnic majority — as the vehicle of instruction, it was also recognized that the resentment of Spanish-Americans is more commonly directed against discrimination and against lower status than against the English language. Either a Spanish-speaking teacher or aide was assigned to each class, and children were free to speak and write in either language, or both, as often happened.

The Hughes model for language training might be described as a "natural" method of language teaching, systematized and accelerated. A child learns language "naturally" by interacting with an adult who uses models of many syntactical elements in his speech and who responds to the child's remarks in such a way as to extend the child's language. The child processes what he hears and derives rules or generalizations which he then tries out. If a mother says to her three-year-old, "Find Daddy and tell him supper is ready," the child does not say to his father, "Find Daddy and tell him supper is ready." He does not repeat verbatim what he has heard, but because of previous exposures to various grammatical forms, he is able to transform his mother's utterance to, "Daddy, Mommy says supper's ready." Even the child's errors reveal his knowledge of grammar: the child who says "He's got morether" has figured out the rule for forming comparatives; he simply doesn't know all the rules and all the exceptions.

To learn a language "naturally" children must hear many examples of well-formed sentences. Furthermore, these must be directed *to him,* so that he will interact with the ideas expressed and, in turn, react to the speaker with his own utterances. Passive listening, as in viewing TV, is not enough; the child must be actively engaged in listening to the speaker and processing what he is saying. When the conversation is two-way, the child is inevitably involved.

In the Hughes program, the teacher consciously supplies the child with examples of grammatical elements at a level of sophistication suitable for him and then reinforces the child for his attempts to practice new syntactical discoveries and for his increased linguistic awareness. This is what is meant by a "natural" method of language teaching, systematized and accelerated.

To stimulate language, children in the Hughes program engage in varied activities including trips, cooking, observation of animals, and physical science experiments. A child's remarks about these experiences are recorded by the teacher, an assistant, or the child himself, with all errors and deficiencies included. A program assistant who serves as a resource person or agent of change helps the teacher to analyze the sample and plan subsequent steps. When the child's story is reread, the teacher, in conversation directed toward the child, includes utterances to serve as a model of the next higher level of language sophistication, asks questions to elicit the more sophisticated phrasing, and praises the child for his accomplishments. The aim is to give the child a "language lift."

## Providing a Language Lift

Let us see how a "language lift" might be provided in a classroom. The children in a first grade immersed a sponge in water and observed the bubbles of air coming out of the sponge. "Coming bubbles out of the sponge," Bertha said excitedly. Her classmates' remarks and hers were recorded by the teaching assistant. The program assistant and the teacher decided in conference that the next language level for Bertha might be the insertion of the subject in a sentence and use of a participle to describe the bubbles. Accordingly, the teacher planned to model this type of construction for Bertha the next day.

Six-by-eight cards were prepared, with each child's remarks printed on an individual card, and with such phrases as "Bertha said" or "Angie remarked" prefacing what the child had said. The plan was to have the teacher read the cards verbatim and then model the correct structure for Bertha. The teacher might say, "I saw bubbles coming out of the sponge, also," and then proceed, by questioning, to elicit the use of the correct structure from the child. The same kind of language mediation is used in all aspects of curriculum work. Classrooms are full of "talking" murals with pictures and accompanying comments, individual books children have made containing pictures and their spontaneous remarks about a particular experience, and collections of stories by the whole class about a common experience.

## Provoking Sentence Transformations

Growth in language control and development of logical thinking can go hand in hand, especially if the child's environment provides for language growth and intellectual development to be mutually stimulating. For example, certain forms of speech like the past tense are best learned as the adult reminisces with the child about an earlier experience, such as a trip to the park. If the experiences were stimulating to the senses, there is also a chance to acquire adjectives, adverbs, or adjectival or adverbial phrases. Such verbalization of past experiences provokes a variety of sentence transformations and provides practice in talking about objects or events no longer present, a skill disadvantaged children often lack. (The reader will recall that both Moore and Sigel have commented upon the disadvantaged child's inability to use the language of reference and to discuss things in the abstract, skills highly important to school learning.)

If the remembering practice is directed systematically by a discriminating adult, it will also involve such skills as sequencing, associating, and categorizing. Children are helped to recall details in chronological order and record them in sequence — a skill highly important in learning to read, where anticipation of what might happen next helps one to figure out new words. It is a skill that also helps in making predictions. Children in one second grade peeled an avocado, ate the fruit, and planted the seed. Not only was there deliberate retrieval of the experience by rereading the books they wrote about their experiences, but, along with the recall, they discussed what was going to happen — what changes might occur in the avocado — recorded the predictions, and played them back during the next few weeks to check predictions.

Much use is also made in the program of categorizing and associating. To develop these skills, teachers ask certain types of questions: (a) Questions about the characteristics of objects children are observing in terms of shape, color and size. There are many opportunities for comparison: "It's bigger than my hand," or "It's smaller than my fingernail." (b) Questions about the origin of an object: Where did it come from? Is it manmade or natural? (c) Questions about the relation of the object to other objects: What do we use it for? How is it used? How it smells — its sensory characteristics. (d) Questions about tastes, or the way something feels, also provoke language. Responses to these discussion-type questions are recorded and sometimes form the basis for a group story:

We tasted clams.

Frank B. said, "We get clams from the ocean."

Sandy said, "Minced means that it's cut in little pieces."

Jose said, "It smells like fish."

Xavier said, "It tastes like meat."

Sally said, "It's salty. It tastes like fish."

## The Teacher's Role

Of paramount importance in accelerating children's acquisition of language is the teacher's consciousness of her role as a modeler of language and her awareness of the syntactic structure of language.

The analysis of language in the Tucson model is based upon a grammatical analysis developed by John Carroll (1964). In this analysis are listed certain sentence types which are basic English expressions. One such type is the *There + a verb phrase*, plus a nominal (a noun, or a word used as a noun). This type of expression simply asserts the existence of something: "There's a rabbit." Another basic type is the *predication* type, where the basic pattern includes a subject and predicate. The constructions include:

A linking verb plus a nominal ("It was Tuesday").

A linking verb plus an adjective ("Her mother is sick").

A linking verb with an adverbial telling *where, when,* etc. ("He's home").

An intransitive verb taking no object ("He's swimming").

A transitive verb plus an object ("He killed a rabbit").

The predication types in particular are useful in studying the language used in the children's stories. The types are used in "kernel" sentences which are then transformed by adding, deleting, transposing word order, or negating.

Grammarians have stated the rules to account for every possible English sentence derived from the kernels. The transformational rules fall into four major types:

1. Addition or expansion.

   For example: "I saw the sick boy" has two additions to the transitive verb + object kernel: addition of the past tense (or change to the past tense); addition of the adjective "sick" which could be expressed in another statement.

2. Deletion or reduction.

   For example, the child might reply to a question asking if he had ever been to a particular location before, "Yes, I was," meaning "Yes, I was there."

3. Transposition.

   For example, a question "Are you ready?" is derived by permutation from the predication type 2, "You are ready." Sentence inversion is another example. One can say, "Those dogs I like," rather than "I like those dogs."

4. Negation.

   An existence assertion can be negated by saying, "There isn't anyone here," instead of "There is someone here." Each of the basic predication types may be similarly negated.

It takes only a little reflection to perceive that a combination of these transformational processes accounts for some of our most complex forms of expression. For example, the participle "curled" in the sentence "I saw the snake curled in the corner" is an addition to the sentence "I saw the snake" (predication type 5); it also represents a deletion in that only one sentence can then do the work of a possible second, "It was curled in the corner."

In addition to analyzing how children are putting sentences together, and what help they may need in transforming kernels to the negative or other forms, the program assistant and teacher also look to see how various parts of speech are used. Does the child use articles like "a" or "the"? Does he use nouns alone (snake), or does he attach adjective modifiers (*long, skinny, green* snake)?

Does he use prepositions correctly to denote relations of space, time, or logical position? Does he use auxiliary verbs?

As the reader can see, the grammatical analysis is not a difficult or complicated one to make. It does serve to make clear the extent and manner of the children's restriction in language at school entrance. As a result of making such analyses, the teacher becomes aware in a very specific way of children's language difficulties and concerned about doing something about them.

The grammatical analysis also helps the teacher to know what grammatical forms to model for the child. She becomes sophisticated in determining what might be done further to provide a "language lift," that is, to increase the complexity of language and to use more transformations. Becoming aware of the discrepancy between how the child is performing and how he should be performing through analyses of his language expression is a necessary first step in teacher modification of language behavior.

To summarize, the Hughes model may be described as based upon the following premises:

1. Interesting curriculum activities, like trips and experiences with cooking food, can provide the stimulus to get children to talk.
2. Under conditions of positive reinforcement, children will increase their use of the English language.
3. The child's own language output in the form of stories dictated to the teacher or to a tape recorder can serve to stimulate the child to talk and also serve as a source of feedback to the child on how well he is doing.
4. Fall and spring comparisons of dictated stories or tapes help teacher and child feel progress and thus serve as reinforcement.
5. Teachers will be more aware of specific needs in language training if they have a knowledge of how language is structured.
6. Teachers can use their knowledge of how language is structured to make diagnoses of pupil needs and plan specific activities to improve language.

## The Program in Action

The raw materials essential to the analysis of language are contained in the dictated stories of the children. But how do we get children to the point of wanting to dictate a story? Let us consider the case of Jose, a first grader, who has just entered school. The first step toward helping a child want to tell something is to provide him with an interested and sympathetic listener. It is also important to structure the environment so that Jose has stimuli to which he can respond. The teacher or the aide, in turn, can listen to anything Jose has to say and can respond to his verbal initiative with comments and questions that invite Jose to explore further and to verbalize more. The adults must be careful to couch their verbal response to the child so as to encourage further exploration of ideas.

Structuring the environment in Jose's case included posting on the classroom door where Jose might see it a large printed chart with big red and yellow apples on it. The teacher read the chart to the class: "Good morning, boys and girls. Today we will taste apples."

They tasted apples but not until everyone looked at them, touched them, smelled them, and told about seeing apple blossoms. Some had even climbed an apple tree. Then they cut into the apple and discovered its texture, juiciness, and degree of sweetness or tartness, all of which provoked language. The verbal interaction was guided by an adult who modeled more complex language forms and a more discriminating vocabulary in answer to children's responses.

The next day Jose discovered on the classroom wall his picture of the apples accompanied by a speech balloon with his own comments such as: "Jose said: Apples good. I like." Comments of other children were also included in speech balloons above their pictures, making a giant "talking" mural. The mural was not resisted as textbooks might be, and children read their own balloons and those of friends with great interest, following a reading by the teacher. In fact, the children seemed hardly aware of whether the teacher read it to them or whether they read it themselves, so closely were they identified with the experience.

Soon a new mural appeared about going to the store to buy apples and sugar for the applesauce to be made. The "applesauce" mural was later reorganized into a big book, which the children read and reread in the library center.

Another day, as the children examined photos of a trip to the park and listened to the taped record of their conversation about the ducks on the pond, Jose suggested it ought to become a mural or a book and offered to do some illustrations.

In sum, what the teacher does is to plan carefully so that experiences like a walk, a trip, or cooking, involving tasting, smelling, or feeling, provoke intellectual involvement and give rise to verbalization. Experiences are used for both intellectual stimulation and language development. The goals or desired outcomes of experiences have been organized under such headings as "Developing Sensory Awareness" and "Building a Concept of Time." Under each heading, experiences have been outlined to lead to acquisition of the goals. Goals and experiences for the two categories of sensory awareness and time are listed below.

## Experiences to Arouse and Express Sensory Perceptions

1. Call attention to how different foods smell and to the smell of cooking food.
2. Provide cooking experiences. Call attention to:
   a. The feel of dough.
   b. The stickiness of jelly.
   c. The sound and sight of things boiling.
   d. The feel of heat from the oven.
   e. The feel and taste of ice cream on the tongue.
3. Have children describe auditory, visual, or tactile stimuli.
   a. The sounds of different animals.
   b. The feel of windblown sand.
4. Have children study and imitate movements.
   a. The movement of a cow as compared to a deer.
   b. The movement of a turtle or fox, etc.
   c. The movement of the wind in the trees.
   d. The working of machines.
5. Have children describe reactions to shared experiences. "The monkeys made us laugh." "When the bull started to get up, I got back."
6. Have children describe personal feelings about experiences.
   a. Physical state after climbing a hill.

b. How one's stomach feels on a bumpy road. Example: The road goes up; my stomach goes up. The road goes down; my stomach goes down."

## Experiences to Develop an Awareness of Time

1. Use walking trips.
   a. Record starting time of walk. Compare with returning time.
   b. Decide what time the group must start back. Let one or two children be the "clock watchers." (This is a good way to allow the child who can tell time to use his skill and give status to time-telling at the same time.)
   c. Look for clocks, calendars, etc., in public places.
   d. Reconstruct what happened on the walk by reading the conversations recorded by the teacher during the walk. "What was happening when Mary said this?"
   e. Put the events of the walk in a time sequence.
   f. Watch the traffic lights or a policeman directing traffic. Observe the timing.
   g. Plan to visit the home of a child at a certain time. Perhaps an invitation could ask the children to come at one o'clock. Decide when to start to get there on time.
2. Use bus trips.
   a. Plan to meet the bus at a certain time. Record the time. Be sure that everyone is ready to go at that time. Make being on time a group affair.
   b. Observe and point out signs which give the opening and closing times of public places — museums, stores, etc.
   c. Ask the custodian, farmer, etc., which jobs must be done daily, weekly, etc.
   d. Point out the schedules kept by trains, buses, and planes. Discuss why they run on schedule.
   e. Record the time of departure and return. Figure out how long the trip took.
   f. Plan ahead for the trip. Mark off the days on the calendar. Make and carry out plans for the trip.
   g. Anticipate what to see and do.

h. Establish a time orientation for the trip. "We *are going* on the trip *tomorrow*." "*Today* is the day for our trip." "We *went* on a trip yesterday."

i. Reconstruct parts of the trip in one or more ways — talking about it, dramatic play, drawing pictures, etc.

j. Take pictures of the trip. Have children arrange them in time sequence and write about each one.

k. Observe the speed of the bus. "Is it going fast or slow?" "When does it go faster or slower?" "What is faster?" "How do we know?"

l. Let the children know that prior arrangements must be made before a trip. The teacher may say, "I went out to Sabino Canyon Sunday. There is a stream where we can wade," or, "If we are going to take a lunch, we will have to make sandwiches. When shall we do that?"

m. Use a trip to a museum or other spot which has "old things" to help the child become aware of the historical past: the "olden days."

3. Use cooking experiences.

a. Time the cooking or baking. Read the time from the recipe. Set the timer. Then check it by the clock. Does it go off at the expected time?

b. Experiment: Cook something too long or not long enough. What happens?

c. Point out the necessity for planning ahead. What utensils will we need? What supplies will we need to get?

There are many other facets of the Hughes program that might be described — how intellectual competencies other than those mentioned are developed through the medium of language; how the children learn to read; what the impact of the program is upon children's motivation and self-image. And, since all facets of the program are relevant to language, much that would have a bearing on the subject matter of this volume has been omitted. It is hoped, however, that the theory underlying the model is complete enough to be helpful to teachers seeking to develop promising practices in language training through the "natural" method.

For teachers who would like to know more about which grammatical elements to model for children, the following list is included. It has been prepared by Dr. Ursula Bellugi-Klima, a psycholinguist, and Dr. Wilbur Hass, developmental psychologist. They have selected elements *roughly* in order of their emergence in child language, although our knowledge of developmental sequence is still extremely limited.

## Grammatical Elements to Model for Young Children

**INFLECTIONS**

Labov notices an absence of a number of inflections which have appeared in the speech of children under five years of age. Perhaps some of these should be considered: possessives, plurals, past tense endings, third person singular present indicative.

**POSSESSIVES**

Show me the pencil's point.
The spoon's handle is plastic.

**PLURALS**

The rocks are rough.
The rubber objects can stretch.

**REGULAR PAST TENSE**

These objects floated in the water.
You counted the number of blocks.

**THIRD PERSON SINGULAR PRESENT INDICATIVE**

The rubber band stretches.
The bird sits on the branch.

**PREPOSITIONS**

Put the triangle next to the square.
Put the triangle behind the square.
Put the triangle in front of the square.

Put the penny between the corks.
Put the penny among the corks.

To test for comprehension of prepositions, one might need to set up the materials in a particular way. For "between-among" distinction, one would need two corks on the one side and more than two corks on the other, for example.

### MODALS IN DECLARATIVE SENTENCES

You must use the spoon to stir it.
We would blow up the balloon this way.

### MODALS AND "DO" WITH NEGATIVES

These objects can't be eaten.
You don't have to stir it.

### "BE" — NEGATIVE AND QUESTION

Labov outlines some patterns of nonstandard Negro speech. Differences may occur in the shape of the negative. For example, he cites the following from children: "It don't all be her fault." "He ain't here." "He ain't start it." "Ain't that a shame?" If these are to be included in the study, the full range of subjects should be used.

This object is not round.
I am not going to suggest what to do today.

The above could also be presented in contracted form "isn't, aren't" to correspond to the so-called negative question.

Isn't this object round?
Aren't you going to work this morning?

### "BE" WITH PAST TENSE

Use a range of subjects: I, you, he, she, it, we, they, noun phrase singular, noun phrase plural.

#### "Be" Past

The papers were wet.
They were all floating before.

#### "Be" Past Negative

These pieces were not shaved.    (weren't)
We weren't looking at round objects yesterday.

#### "Be" Past Question (Affirmative and Negative)

Weren't crystals put into this jar?
Wasn't this one of the floating objects?

## YES/NO QUESTIONS

The children in the Tucson study asked well-formed yes/no questions — with auxiliary verb and inverted subject — by the time they were five. One could elicit such questions from the children with a "20 questions" game. Suppose the children have a collection of objects in front of them. The teacher might say: "I'm thinking of one of these objects and you have to find out which one. Ask questions that I can answer by saying yes or no." The children should first name all the objects. The teacher can play the role of questioner when the child has an object in mind. In keeping with the discovery of properties of objects, one should not use the object name; thus, "Is it round?" not "Is it a button?"

### With Modal Auxiliary Verbs

Can you blow it up?
Wouldn't this be used for eating?

### With "Do"

Do you use these for writing?
Does this animal have a long neck?

A variation of this game would be to have the children *answer* the questions with respect to a particular array of objects. The child has one object in mind:

| Teacher: | Child: |
|---|---|
| Does the object have round edges? | No, it is not a button or a ring. |
| Does the object have paper around it? | No, it is not the crayon. |
| Does the object have a sharp point? | No, it is not the thumbtack. |
| Does the object grow in nature? | Yes, it is the bean. |

### "BE" — AFFIRMATIVE AND QUESTION

Labov has outlined some sources of reading problems for Negro speakers of nonstandard English. One of these is the general absence of the copula in sentences.

This spoon is plastic.
They are all round objects.

Probably it is preferable to use the full form of the copula, although it is ordinarily contracted in colloquial speech. Using the full form shows the relationship to yes/no questions more clearly. Compare the following:

| | |
|---|---|
| He's coming. | We're finished. |
| Is he coming? | We are finished. |
| He is coming. | Are we finished? |

Question forms of the above set of sentences show the full form of the copula. For example:

Is this spoon plastic?
Are you looking at the round objects?

### INDIRECT QUESTIONS

These were mastered by the children in the Tucson study. Labov notes that in embedded questions in nonstandard speech he stuc'' word order of original question is preserved, as in: "I don't know how did I do it."

He doesn't know how he can do it; perhaps you can help him.
Tell your partner where he should put the round ones.
(others with how, why, what, when, where, who)

### "WH" QUESTIONS

Use different interrogative words — who, what, where, when, why, how, which — and a variety of auxiliary verbs — be, do, have, modals — and some negative questions.

Which objects are made of two materials?
How could you guess which ones will float?

These can be elicited as a two-person game. Suppose we take the collection of objects on page 112. Child A thinks of an object and must answer questions. Child B must ask what, where, who questions. Example: B, "Where could you find this object?" A, "Out of doors." B, "How big is it?" (Answer with respect to the array.) A, "It is small." B, "What can you do with it?" A, "You can eat it." B, "It must be the bean."

### TAG QUESTIONS

You can grind it, can't you?
You don't need more, do you?

### COORDINATIONS

Put the cork and the button in the water.

You can observe gases, and she can study liquids.

### ADVERSATIVES

This is tall but light.

I am thinking of an object which is dark but not heavy.

### DISJOINT

Pick out either the large ones or the dark ones.

I can use large ones or small ones.

### COMPARATIVES

These are rather late in appearance, in terms of cognitive structures (see Sinclair-de-Zwart, 1969) and syntactic structures.

Find the shinier piece.

Touch the pile which has the bigger pieces in it.

(also higher, clearer, tighter, looser, fuller, smarter, prettier, softer, harder, etc.)

Find the one that is clearer and lower.

### COMPLEX NOUN PHRASE

The children in the Tucson study used nouns with one modifier and perhaps also a determiner. More complex noun phrases were rarely used. Requirements of these tasks include precise description and definition of properties of objects. This can be incorporated into a complex noun phrase. Describe objects by properties, without using names.

Show me the long, red object.

Give me the short, narrow piece.

These descriptions, or variations on them, such as "Find the one which is short and narrow," can be elicited. Two children work in pairs, separated by a screen, but each with the same array of materials in front of him. Child A must describe each material or object so that the other child can identify it. Restriction: no names, only description of properties.

### COMPLEX AUXILIARY VERB PHRASE

Use more than one auxiliary verb per main sentence. These could be elicited by asking children to describe games to another child so that he could play. "Hide and Seek," "Dodge Ball," "Tag," "Red Light, Green Light," and "Scissors, Paper, Rock" are all excellent for this.

This liquid could be made thinner.

You might have sorted them like this.

## PASSIVES

Use full passives of the type "The cat was chased by the dog" and colloquial passives, "This cup got broken."

The ice will be melted quickly by the heat.

These objects were found out of doors.

## AFFIXAL NEGATION

This is a later-appearing development in the speech of the children studied.

Some of you may be unable to finish today.

The yarn was partly unwound.

## NEGATION WITH INDEFINITES

The children in the Tucson study did not have all the rules for the relation of negative and indefinite even at a rather late period. In addition, Labov notes that negative sentences with indefinites have special variants in nonstandard Negro dialects. He notes sentences like "He don't know nobody," "Ain't nobody see it," and others. Notice the location of the negative — whether it is connected with the auxiliary verb of the sentence or not — and the relationship of negative and indefinite forms — no, none, nobody, nothing, never, any, anybody, anywhere, anytime, etc.

### Negative before Auxiliary Verb

None of these is round.

These animals never fly in the air.

### Negative with Auxiliary and Indefinite after

I don't see anything that is round.

He doesn't know anybody in the room yet.

### Other

This watch has no hands.

This animal hasn't any fur, and neither does this one.

**RELATIVE CLAUSES**

Whatever objects you find can be used.

It's the round buttons that should be put in piles of light or dark.

**TEMPORAL CONNECTIVES**

Use before, after, when, as soon as, etc. Rearrange order of parts of sentence. If necessary, teach meaning with simple situations first. These occur very late in the developmental sequence and perhaps should not be used unless the children are rather advanced.

Before you begin the game, choose a partner.

Raise your hand as soon as you have tried them all.

**CAUSAL CONNECTIVES**

You may need to teach meaning of "because."

The balloon gets bigger because it is being filled with air.

Put the dark ones here and the light ones there, because we want to sort the objects.

**CONDITIONAL STATEMENTS**

Remember that the clauses can occur either before or after the main proposition without changing the meaning. Try both ways.

If this piece floats, then try the larger one.

Don't take the piece out unless it floats.

## References

Carroll, John. 1964. *Language and thought.* Englewood Cliffs, N.J.: Prentice-Hall.

Sinclair-de-Zwart, H. 1969. Developmental psycholinguistics. In D. Elkind and J. H. Flavell, eds., *Studies in cognitive development: Essays in honor of Jean Piaget.* New York: Oxford University Press.

# 6

## COURTNEY B. CAZDEN

# Language Programs for Young Children: Notes from England and Wales[1]

In the spring of 1969 I spent four weeks in England and Wales. I was especially interested in children three to eight years old; in children we call disadvantaged for reasons of poverty or discrimination; in what English nursery or infant schools which express the philosophy of the Plowden Report[2] are doing to aid language development; and in what people in schools or universities think they ought to be doing. What follows is a set of 11 separate notes on observations and conversations and my reactions as an American to what I saw and heard and read. The purpose is not a comprehensive account of even one aspect of education in England and Wales. That would be arrogant to attempt and impossible to accomplish after only four weeks, even when supplemented by previous visits (Cazden, 1968; Cazden and Williams, 1969). Instead, I've tried to use the English experience to highlight ideas and practices here.[3]

[1] The trip on which these observations were made was supported by a grant from the Ford Foundation for a survey and analysis of preschool language programs in the United States. An earlier draft of this report was sent to all the people I visited in England and Wales with a request for suggestions and criticisms. This version incorporates all comments received through December 1969. I am grateful for their help.

[2] The Plowden Report is the official English blueprint for primary education: nursery, infant and junior schools through age 11. Cited in the reference list as Great Britain Central Advisory Council for Education (1967), the two-volume study was the work of a committee of Her Majesty's government headed by Lady Plowden.

[3] For comparative discussions of language education for older children in the United States and Great Britain, see Dixon (1967) for the report of an English-

Because I am writing these notes after working on a summer project
to train kindergarten teachers for American Indian schools, jointly
sponsored by the Bureau of Indian Affairs and the National Association for the Education of Young Children, some of the examples
from the United States are taken from this context. The 11 notes are
titled:

> Extending Children's Language
> Peer-Group Talk
> Individual Daily Schedules
> Reinforcement for What?
> Standard English: To Teach or Not to Teach
> Use of Local Cultural Content
> Bilingualism in School and Out
> Communication Skills
> The Language of Children's Written Sentences
> The Gahagan-Bernstein Educational Program
> Compensatory Education

## Extending Children's Language

Margaret Roberts, head of the diploma course in child development
at the University of London Institute of Education, describes good
teaching as "sensitive observation" which will lead to a high quality
of "mental companionship" between teacher and child which in turn
will "extend" the child's ideas and language. These are her words:
sensitive observation, mental companionship, and extension. They
express the general belief of English infant school educators (and
many of their American colleagues) that language development
should be nourished by the teacher in the context of the child's work
and play.

Such informal nourishment is contrasted with more formal lessons in which something preselected by the teacher is taught to a
child or group of children. I heard several objections to such lessons.
Miss E. M. Parry, inspector of nursery and infant schools in Bristol,
objected to the content. She contrasted English infant school prac-

man on the bi-national (1967) Dartmouth Seminar; and see Squire and Applebee (1969) for the report of observations by Americans on secondary school.

tices with one American preschool classroom she had visited as a member of the Plowden Commission. The concept *heavy* was being taught, one of five concepts for that day. The teacher evidently taught by rote, through words alone, and didn't use blocks or other materials available in the classroom to give the children concrete, personal experience with *heaviness*. Few would disagree with Miss Parry that such superficial verbal instruction is bad teaching. But one can argue that structured language programs could do much better.

Other educators object because structured programs are pre-planned by the teacher in content (and therefore do not flow from children's interests) or in timing (and therefore interrupt or conflict with the child's concerns at the moment). Here one can argue that children's interests can be aroused as well as followed, and that any child can tolerate some interruptions to his work as long as the school day also contains blocks of time which he can plan.

The key word in England is "extension." What does this word imply? Does it really happen? What kind of knowledge or awareness does a teacher need to do it successfully?

At the least, the concept of "extension" implies a direction. In what direction do we want to extend children's language? This is another way of asking a critical question: in any particular situation, what kind of language, what ways of communicating, are of greatest worth? Unless teachers have given serious thought to this question, it seems unlikely that they will be aware of the most important directions for help. As Mr. Norfield, head (principal) of the John Milton Primary School in the Batterseapark area of London put it, if the teacher is not aware of particular aspects of experience, she can't pay attention to them; if she's not aware of the intellectual skills and concepts inherent in the simplest activity, she cannot nourish those skills and concepts in the context of the child's play.

According to Benita Jackson, nursery and infant school inspector in the London dock area of Newham and member of the Nuffield Foundation mathematics team, it is generally accepted that infant school teachers need knowledge about mathematics. Consider the treatment of symmetry in *Beginnings,* one of the Nuffield booklets for teachers: "Although no observations may come from the children at this stage, it is useful for the teacher to have a knowledge of symmetry when patterns are being made in the sand and a variety of differently shaped containers are being used. . . . The most important aspect of this work is to encourage in children an awareness of the shapes and patterns around them. This is simply a matter of focusing attention for a few moments, and introducing the necessary vocabulary so that the children can describe what they see" (Nuffield Foundation, 1967, pp. 4, 89). Things can be symmetrical in different ways, and *Beginnings* gives examples of patterns that are the same back to front or upside down (reflection), moving along (translation), and round and round (rotation).

Without understanding these concepts herself, the teacher cannot ask the best question, offer the most pertinent equipment, focus the child's attention on the relevant examples. In short, she can only start from where the child is and then help him learn something new if she knows about exciting places to go. Cremin said as much in his analysis of the progressive movement in the United States:

For the resourceful teacher, all activities and occupations had an instrumental as well as an intrinsic value; they afforded opportunity for social and intellectual growth as well as more immediate satisfaction to the children.

But there is a point to be made here, one that Dewey argued for the rest of his career but never fully communicated to some who thought themselves his disciples. A teacher cannot know which opportunities to use, which impulses to encourage, or which social attitudes to cultivate without a clear sense of what is to come later. With respect to intellect this implies a thorough acquaintance with organized knowledge as represented in the disciplines. To recognize opportunities for early mathematical learning, one must know mathematics. . . . In short, the demand on the teacher is twofold: thorough knowledge of the disciplines and an awareness of those common experiences of childhood that can be utilized to lead children toward the understanding represented by this knowledge (Cremin, 1961, p. 138).

It is easy for us as teachers to admit that we need to know more about mathematics. But because we all talk, we assume that we're all experts on language. The trouble is that the knowledge about language we require as teachers is one level beyond using it ourselves, no matter how richly we may do so. We need to know *about* language; we need to be aware of its structure and functions, self-consciously and analytically. We need to understand the value of differentiated vocabulary in perception and memory (i.e., of different kinds of symmetrical patterns); we need to know what Mrs. Tough is finding out about the ways different children use language to convey information (see later note on communication skills); we need to be aware of how we as teachers use language (Barnes et al., 1969); we need to wrestle with "notions of theory construction and rational discussion" (O'Neil, 1969, p. 363).[4] And then we have to plan how to use that knowledge in the classroom.

But even if we had such knowledge, it is not certain that a busy infant school teacher can do much extending of children's oral language when there are so many other demands on her time. I talked about this to Miss S. Ena Grey, Welsh member of the Plowden Commission and organizer of infant education for the county of Glamorgan. We were at an exhibit of play corners made for nursery and infant schools as part of the two-year course for "nursery nurses" (nursery school assistants) at the Bridgend Technical College in Wales. The corners were constructed and equipped very realistically: post office, cafe, gas station, hospital, hairdresser, sweet shop, fish and chip shop, and a ranch and Indian tepee (imported from the United States via TV).

Miss Grey felt that these play corners stimulated play, and thereby language, if the teacher took an active part in promoting play through provision of materials and through her participation as well. "The teacher shouldn't just say to herself, 'Well, there are five children happily occupied and I can ignore them.'" On the other hand, she may sometimes have to ignore them while she takes advantage of the opportunity to work with other children in reading or number work. Thus, there are conflicting pulls on the teacher's time: to participate and thereby extend the child's experience in these play corners, or to use the time elsewhere.

Given the pressures infant school teachers feel to get around to each child in a group of 40 with help in reading, other activities may

[4] See Cazden, 1970, for a discussion of objectives in early childhood language education both in England and the United States.

understandably not get the attention they deserve. One teacher of a five- and six-year-old group in the Sea Mills Infant School in Britsol spent ten minutes of her morning as follows:

Writes a story for a girl. Writes a story for another girl, talking it over before writing anything down. Time out to point out word in a dictionary for a girl. Writes story for another girl. Monitors other children in classroom, calling softly to a girl standing near the milk table, "Judy, if you're not having milk, come away from that table." Helps dictionary girl with another word. Gets up to to help boy decide what to do. Redirects three children out of the coat room. Gives word to dictionary girl. Gets box out of desk and says, "Listen, please. If anyone would like to buy a jam tart, come and get one." Checks one girl's original story. Checks another girl's story and tells her to write her name. Checks whose milk is left on the table: "Who had a bottle of milk and didn't finish it?" Goes back to write two more stories. Asks Simon to get his very first book and his most recent book and show them to the visitor.

It is not possible to say whether this is representative behavior. Furthermore, the conversations which the above record simply lists as happening could be very valuable. Wireless recording equipment would be needed in order to record the content of those conversations for subsequent analysis. But as Denis and Judy Gahagan, who developed Basil Bernstein's educational program, point out, even that is not enough: "We actually tried this at the S.R.U. [Sociological Research Unit] and our finding was that it does give you a measure of 'how much' talk, *but* unless it is accompanied minimally by written observations, it is frequently impossible to identify the person to whom the talk is being directed, and worse still, it is often impossible to understand the speech in the sense of knowing what is being talked *about,* because of the use of referents such as 'this,' 'these,' 'its,' 'them,' and of many personal pronouns. The ideal solution is, of course, to use video tape" (personal communication, 1969). Careful observation is also necessary to make sure that teachers do, in fact, talk to the children who need help most and are not monopolized by children who are already the most verbal. The Gahagans met this problem too; see the section on the Gahagan-Bernstein program for their solution.

Two research projects now under way in England should help us understand better what kinds of communication take place in English primary schools. When Miss Parry retired from Bristol on 31 August 1969, she began an 18-month project, sponsored by the Schools Council and based at the Rachel McMillan College in London, to document the best practices in nursery and infant schools. And Brian Simon of the University of Leicester is analyzing verbal interaction in classrooms where children work alone and in small groups (*Times Educational Supplement,* 2 May 1969).

## Peer-Group Talk

Children do learn from each other. That's one of the implications of the Coleman Report on educational opportunity in the United States (Coleman et al., 1966; Jencks, 1969). Coleman found that the one characteristic of a disadvantaged child's school which had a demonstrable effect on his achievement was the composition of the peer group. When achievement is measured by tests of verbal ability (which were more sensitive to school differences than other achievement tests), a disadvantaged child benefits from going to school with middle-class children. One source of that benefit may be the quality of peer-group talk (though other sources are possible, such as the quality of the lessons planned by the teacher). Although attempts in the United States to support that hypothesis in preschools integrated by social class have so far brought inconclusive or disappointing results (e.g. Karnes, 1969), the idea continues to appeal.

It seems intuitively obvious that the amount of peer-group conversation that takes place in English infant schools is superior for language development to the enforced silence of many primary school classrooms in the United States. At least there's no negative, repressive effect. In keeping with Coleman's findings, it also seems that vertical (mixed-age or "family") grouping would make that conversation even more beneficial. (English teachers and heads are very articulate about their rationale for grouping. They may not agree with each other, but each head knows exactly why she groups as she does. In many schools new five-year-olds are not segregated in a reception class but instead are mixed with sixes or with sixes and sevens, so that they can be inducted into the school culture by their slightly older peers.)

Because of all the foregoing, I was especially interested in the quality of peer-group talk. Basil Bernstein said he had been told, "You should hear them talk in the Wendy House" (the English playhouse or doll corner). Bernstein eavesdropped on conversations in Wendy Houses as part of his study of the language of five- to seven-year-old children (Bernstein and Henderson, 1969; Bernstein and Young, 1967; Hawkins, 1969; Robinson and Rackstraw, 1967). He heard children talking all right, but he concluded that language in that setting consists mainly of highly routinized, well-rehearsed bits of previously learned responses, or response types, which probably do little to extend language development (Bernstein, personal communication, 1969).

I eavesdropped, too, on the conversation in a Wendy House in a nursery school for children three to five years old. Four girls were talking as they played. Girl 1 was in the doll bed, pretending to be crying like a baby. Girl 2 and Girl 3 were with her and Girl 4 entered later. Following is a ten-minute record, taken down in written notes (not by tape recorder). A line (————) indicates words I couldn't hear.

Girl 2. Baby! (slapping Girl 1) Baby, don't cry. I'll get ————.

Girl 3. (Goes over, sits down, and feeds Girl 1) ———— right? Go to sleep!

Girl 3. Who are you? You're not coming into our house (said to Girl 4 who appeared at the door).

Girl 2. She's coming in!

Girl 3. Get up. Let Mommy ————. OK? Get up. Let Mommy put ————. Get into bed. I'll cover you up. Lay down. Come on, Ann. Look after your baby. (Girls 2 and 3 take a doll carriage and go out. Girls 1 and 4 stay; Girl 1 still in bed.)

Girl 1. Cries.

Girl 3. (Calling from outside) Cheryl, Cheryl, come! (Girl 4 plays alone, looks out the window, ignores Girl 1. Then fixes Girl 1's covers without speaking, starts to sweep the floor. Girl 1 sits up in bed. Girl 3 returns.)

Girl 4. Baby woke up!

Girl 3. ———————————— (exits again).

Girl 4. (To Girl 1) Go sleep. Go sleep. Go sleep (repeated ten times in all). (Girl 1 makes noises, and then gets up.)

This record may be unrepresentative. A child's language undoubtedly *can* be extended by the communicative demands of conversations with peers, whether or not an adult is present. I'm sure such evidence could be found. But the above record provides little assurance that, left alone in even the richest school environment, children will gain in communicative competence more than they would if playing with their peers in an informal group on the playground or street.

## Individual Daily Schedules

In the Bristol classroom described above, all the children who dictated stories to the teacher were girls. That record was taken from 9:28 to 9:38 in the morning. It was 9:55 before the first boy came in from building with blocks out on the patio and sat down to draw or dictate or read. I asked Miss Nash, head of the school, about this. She had taken counts of activities by sex and time of day, and agreed that boys seek more vigorous activity early in the morning and only settle down later to the three R's. There is a definite expectation, at Sea Mills and elsewhere, that each child will do some reading, writing, and arithmetic each day. (This expectation is transmitted more by older to younger children than by explicit direction of the teacher.) But it still leaves each child responsible for selecting the *form* of his work, and the *time* during the day when he will do it. An integrated day can accommodate all kinds of individual schedules, including these striking differences between girls and boys.

## Reinforcement for What?

In the Westfield Infant School in Leicestershire, Rosemary Williams, the head, and I watched a five-year-old boy spend a long time on a collage picture and then take it over to his teacher for her to display. Miss Williams commented on the importance of teachers finding ways to value children's work. "If this isn't done, then children stop working." Valuing may be at the moment, as the above teacher did with the child's collage; it may be in a group evaluation session at the end of the morning, as many of the teachers in Miss Williams' school do; it may be in an even larger group such as the daily assembly, as is done at the Tide Mills Infant School in the Deptford area of London.

Tangible products like paintings, constructions, and written stories can gain recognition in a group session. But the scientific discovery while working with a balance can't; neither can the good question about something seen on the way to school; nor the thoughtful comment about the implications of a story. These have to be valued at the moment or the opportunity is lost. We may believe that intellectual activity should eventually be its own reward, but some children probably need extrinsic reinforcement as well.

In the United States, the Bereiter-Engelmann program has been noted for its use of extrinsic reinforcement. The teacher rewards with a warm smile, a handshake, and verbal praise — "good talking!" (as in the film of Jean Osborne teaching, distributed by the Anti-Defamation League). I know some observers find this practice offensive. I don't. If it's acceptable to say "good worker" to a child who sticks with a job after an initial period of flitting or giving up, why can't we say "good talker" to a child who has been silent in school and is now participating in the ways we expect? After all, reinforcement simply means transmitting our valuing openly to the child.

But what are the ways of talking we expect? My questions about the Bereiter-Engelmann program are more about *what* they reinforce than *how*. Too often "good talking" consists of the right answer to a teacher's question spoken in only one acceptable way. The question "What is this?" has only one answer, and that answer must be given in a set form, "This is a Z," not "That is . . ." or "It is . . ." or anything else. Such talking may be required if one adopts group choral response as a teaching strategy. But it hardly taps the truly human powers of any child's language ability.

Can we find the time and the ways, personally and individually, to value the child's thoughtful and unique verbal responses to his world?

## Standard English: To Teach or Not to Teach

The Schools Council project to develop a language program for children of West Indian origin is directed by Jim Wight. The project coordinators are John Sinclair from the English Department and Philip Taylor from the School of Education of the University of Birmingham. The program is planned for children from seven to nine years old because it is based in part on children's writing. It has two objectives: "to help children to write Standard English — concentrating on the places where the West Indian dialect creates special difficulties for the child; and to improve the oral fluency and general communication skills and confidence of the children — focusing also on intellectual tasks that are fundamental to successful communication at school" (Schools Council Working Paper 29, 1970, p. 7). The first objective will be discussed here and the second in a later note.

In addition to the usual distinction between home language (in this case a Caribbean Creole) and school language (standard English), Wight and Sinclair separate their goals for oral and written language and concentrate their efforts in trying to help children *write* standard forms. According to Wight, no matter how you try to disguise it, if you suggest an alternative way of speaking, you are implicitly suggesting that something is wrong with what the child said in the first place. Moreover, written work is where children receive the most criticism for irregular forms. Listeners tend to ignore grammatical deviations, but the same deviations become glaringly obvious in written compositions. Oral drills are used for oral practice in forms needed in writing. "It is intended that these standard forms should be primarily associated in the child's mind with written English" (Schools Council Working Paper 29, 1970, p. 27).

The project is developing some unusual puzzlelike materials for teaching standard English morphology such as the following for noun and verb agreement:

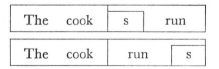

If one adds an *s* to the noun, then the only verb piece that fits is one that cannot itself take an *s*; if the noun is singular, then the matching verb piece has a space which must be filled by an *s*.

At first, it seemed to me inappropriate to use a mnemonic device to teach a linguistic rule. But as Wight pointed out, this rule is a completely arbitrary, meaningless part of our language. If the visual shapes of words can aid learning, why not exploit them? One good thing about the materials is that the original decision is made about the noun: is it plural or singular? Once that decision has been made, the shape of the noun determines the shape, literally, of the verb.

In its approach to standard English, the Birmingham project takes an intermediate position between the extremes of American programs for "teaching English as a second language" on the one hand, and "leave their dialect alone" on the other. Bernstein speaks strongly for the latter, at least for the oral language of preadolescents:

There is nothing, but nothing, in the dialect as such, which prevents a child from internalizing and learning to use universalistic meanings. But if the contexts of learning, the examples, the reading books are not contexts which are triggers for the child's imaginings, are not triggers on the child's curiosity and explorations in his family and community, then the child is not at home in the educational world. If the teacher has to say continuously, "Say it again, darling, I didn't understand you," then in the end the child may say nothing. If the culture of the teacher is to become part of the consciousness of the child, then the culture of the child must first be in the consciousness of the teacher. This may mean that the teacher must be able to understand the child's dialect, rather than deliberately attempting to change it (Bernstein and Henderson, 1969, pp. 15-16).

Three additional arguments in favor of practicing standard English (SE) in written form, as Wight and others suggest, were expressed during discussions at a fall, 1969, conference at the Center for Applied Linguistics in Washington, D.C. First, Orlando Taylor argued for widening the range of pronunciations acceptable as SE to include black English pronunciation as we now include all regional variations, thereby limiting SE to matters of grammatical structure. In print, pronunciation automatically becomes irrelevant. Second, according to Claudia Mitchell Kernan, black students more easily accept the need for writing SE while considering attempts at "proper" speech as affected (Mitchell, 1969). Finally, as we note in more detail below, one of the skills which working-class children most need to practice is communicating ideas explicitly without dependence on gestures or concrete referents. That is the task which written language imposes.

## Use of Local Cultural Content

Infant schools in the dock area of London, on an RAF base in Oxfordshire, and in the industrial midlands of Leicestershire look very much the same. When inside, one loses awareness of the local culture from which the children come. Until very recently, this was also true in the United States. Now beginning adaptations are being made.

For instance, in some kindergartens for American Indian children there will be richer dramatic play, and richer language accompanying it, because the block corner is liberally supplied with cows, sheep, and horses (replacing the zebras and elephants), and with pick-up trucks (like those every Navajo family owns) that are large enough to carry the animals to the trading post or rodeo. Similarly, classroom interaction will gain from a life-size driftwood horse, complete with blanket, saddle, and reins, instead of the culturally neutral equipment of most dramatic play corners. And why not a rodeo lotto game, as Vera John suggests, with different sizes and sexes of animals and different sizes and positions of players? Such a game would require that children express in words those visual discriminations which they have previously learned well in their out-of-school life.

English voices are heard on this subject. Leila Berg is one of them. In *Risinghill* (1968) she writes of the birth and death of a comprehensive secondary school in the Islington section of London with children from nineteen nationalities. This school cherished their differences and created a multicultural program from them. More recently, at the annual conference of the Pre-schools Playgroups Association, Mrs. Berg attacked the middle-class world portrayed in children's readers and the way society is "depersonalizing children from working class homes" (*Times,* 21 April 1969; *Times Educational Supplement,* 25 April 1969). She is herself the author of an alternative set of readers: *Nippers,* published by Macmillan in

England. One paperback primer is called *Fish and Chips for Supper* (Berg, 1968). Basil Bernstein is another voice, criticizing the Plowden Report for overemphasizing universal stages and individual differences while minimizing the implications of subcultural differences (Bernstein and Davies, 1969) and arguing for relevant "contexts of learning." Note that I am talking here about the positive possibilities for curriculum change which these subcultural differences provide, not the negative implications for adjustment to schools as they are which we in America have emphasized in the recent past.

It may be that English society is more homogeneous than ours, and that, therefore, the goal of the cultural pluralism has less meaning. Continued immigration from the Commonwealth countries would make England become more like the United States in this respect. But the restrictive legislation recently passed by Parliament makes that a less immediate prospect. In the United States, demands from minority groups for help in enlarging their cultural identity rather than wiping it out is forcing change in the schools, meager as it is. If, for other reasons, we transplant English practices to our schools for young children, let's not lose what little headway we've gained.

## Bilingualism in School and Out

Language is one important expression of cultural identity, and part of the shift away from a melting pot toward cultural pluralism in the United States is the introduction of bilingual education.[5] In Wales, bilingual education is well established and widespread. About 25 percent of children in Wales learn Welsh as their native language. At school entrance, parents in most areas can select Welsh-speaking schools in which English is introduced as a second language at age eight, or English-speaking schools where Welsh is introduced in the same way. According to Aneurin Williams, research officer of the Welsh Language Unit section of the Schools Council Project in Compensatory Education, some English-speaking parents chose the Welsh-speaking schools because they believe in promoting the Welsh language.

[5] For discussion of bilingualism in Ireland, see Macnamara (1966).

Promotion of the Welsh language is not a matter for schools alone. E. M. Thomas writes in the *Times Educational Supplement* (9 May 1969) about the Welsh Language Society's campaign against road signs printed only in English. Evidently some teachers have been active in this campaign. After a strong statement on behalf of acts which do not violate public opinion even if they violate the law, Thomas urges the local education committees not to take action against these teachers:

I should have thought it is ridiculous that children whose mother tongue is Welsh should grow up hearing one set of placenames on the tongues of their families but always seeing another, English form on road signs and in official use.

The same goes for all the words used in public notices and so forth. What sense does it make for an education committee to teach Welsh in its schools (unless it thinks of it as a dead language) and at the same time show no concern for the public status and use of the language?

One way children's learning in school can be reinforced is by opportunities to use that learning outside of school. If educators truly believe in bilingualism, shouldn't they be campaigning for all possible opportunities to use the second (or first) language? Why not English-Spanish road signs in Texas, and English-Navajo road signs on the reservations in Arizona?

## Communication Skills

K. Lovell of the University of Leeds Institute of Education asked about communication problems of disadvantaged children: Are they the result of particular communication patterns in the home or are they one particular form of a general difference in symbolic functioning? The research of his colleague, Mrs. Joan Tough, strongly suggests the former interpretation.

Mrs. Tough is doing a longitudinal study of the language development of children, half from "favored" and half from "less-favored" backgrounds. These categories are based on the father's occupation and an interview to assess the quality of linguistic fostering provided by the home. Each group of 24 is further divided with half attending nursery school and half at home. *All four subgroups were equated on mean Stanford-Binet IQ* (means = 129, 128.3, 127.5 and 125.3).

At the time I spoke with Mrs. Tough, language samples had been taken and analyzed only at the age of three years. Each child's speech was tape-recorded in a one-hour play session with another child of the subject's choice. In her analysis of the transcriptions of these play sessions, Mrs. Tough is looking for differences predicted by Basil Bernstein's work, but in younger children than he has studied.

Following is a summary of some of the differences in language use of the "favored" versus the "less-favored" children which Mrs. Tough has found (1969):

While the total number of utterances was about the same (even slightly larger for the less favoured group), the relative frequency with which the children talked about particular aspects of their environment was very different. The less favoured children gave nearly three times as many instructions to their peer; the favoured children talked about qualitative attributes, relationships such as causation, the function or purpose of an object, and things recalled from the past or anticipated in the future, from two to seven times as often.

All of the children's "items of representation" (of which the above list is a part) were rated as to whether they required the presence of the concrete situation for effective communication. This "concrete component" constitutes 20.9% of the representations of the favoured children and 34.5% of the representations of the less favoured children. The most frequent forms of the "concrete component" are pronouns whose only reference is to something pointed at in the environment. Such "exophoric" reference is contrasted with "anaphoric" reference, where pronouns refer to an antecedent previously supplied in words. The percentage of anaphoric references (which would communicate without the concrete context) was 22.8% for the favoured children and only 7.7% for the less favoured children. This finding replicates Bernstein's research (as reported in Hawkins, 1969).

Remember that these differences are found among children who are in the same range of scores on the Stanford-Binet. This means that children of equivalent intellectual ability are not equally disposed to use language in particular ways. Being able to communicate information without the support of a concrete context is one such use — required in describing the past, planning for the future, and talking over the telephone, especially to strangers. It is the use of language tapped in the Language Function Test developed by the Wight-Sinclair group at Birmingham, and it is one of the communications skills they hope to improve in their curriculum for West Indian children. It is also a main focus of the Gahagan-Bernstein program.

One of the consultants for the Birmingham project who has been trying out new ideas in communication education is an inspector for junior schools in London, John Welch. Mr. Welch went with a stopwatch to some schools in his area to see how much chance children had to talk. He found, as observers have found in the United States, that in a class discussion at the upper primary level (intermediate grades in the United States), the teacher talked about 70 percent of the time, and six or seven children monopolized the rest. Under such circumstances, most of the children have minimal opportunities for expressing ideas in words. So he started trying out new ideas for classroom organization and activities for oral language development.

One of the teachers with whom Welch has worked is Miss Ternouth, who has nine-year-olds at the Tide Mill Junior School in Deptford, a disadvantaged area in Southeast London. I visited Miss Ternouth's class when her children were working on communication tasks. There were 32 children, divided into pairs or small groups, all working on some kind of talking activity. For example:

Two girls were making puppets for a theater and then going to plan a play.

Two boys sat on either side of a screen, each with plasticene, buttons, and string. One boy was making a face with the materials and giving directions to his partner as he worked so that the two faces would be identical in the end. After they had compared faces, they were to make up a story about them.

Two girls were planning and then painting a mural about a fire.

Four boys were using Lego (construction blocks) to build a village and then would make up a story about the people who live there.

Two girls stood on either side of an easel. One girl was painting a pattern and giving directions to her partner. Then they would evaluate how similar they had been able to make the two patterns.

Because the situation where two children are separated by an opaque screen and forced to communicate information by words alone has been used in communication experiments in the United States, it was especially interesting to see the same idea used in an educational program in England. The idea of using screens in enrichment projects originated in the language propram directed by Gahagan and Gahagan (1970), with whom Welch consulted in the spring of 1966.

The same principle could be applied with preschool children as well. Vera John (personal communication) suggests that after two children have become very familiar with a particular puzzle, they can work together. One child has the frame and the other child has the pieces. By words alone, the child with the frame must ask for the pieces, one by one: "Give me the piece that fits under his neck"; "Give me the big, white one," etc. As with the rodeo lotto game, the task for the child is to translate into language visual discriminations he has already learned to make. But whereas visual information about the rodeo is acquired out of school, visual information about the puzzle is learned in school, but prior to any need for communicating that information in words.

## The Language of Children's Written Sentences

In all the infant schools I visited except one, a child's first reading material consisted of sentences which he made up to accompany his drawings. At first he dictated them to the teacher; gradually he began to copy her writing, either beneath his or on top of it; finally he did the writing himself, with extensive use (in virtually all classrooms) of small picture dictionaries. One school was the exception. In the Lionel Road Primary School in the Brentford borough of outer London, the children read their own sentences, but no handwriting was required. David Mackay and Brian Thompson of the Department of General Linguistics, University College, London, have developed initial literacy materials which separate the conceptual process of sentence composition from the mechanical skill of handwriting. Each child has a word folder with a preselected store of common words plus some blanks for his personal collection. He also has a stand on which words from a folder can be set up as a text. A pilot version of these materials and manual (Thompson, Shaub, and Mackay, 1968) is being tried out in schools all over England. They will be published by Longmans Green in England. Unfortunately, at the time of my visit there were no plans for publication in the United States.

There are many interesting aspects to these materials and to what children do with them. Here I will only comment on three: the kinds of sentences which I saw children dictate or compose; a developmental progression which Mackay and Thompson have discovered in the relation between what children intend to say and what they actually set out on their stands; and what children learn about the structure of their language.

First, the kind of sentences. At the Brize Norton School on an RAF base in Oxfordshire, I visited a classroom of five-year-olds from families of mixed socioeconomic status comparable to the families in the Lionel Road School. The teacher had given each child a new booklet of unlined paper for his drawings and stories, and asked each child to draw a picture and then dictate a story for her to write.

While the children were drawing, I left to watch a BBC educational TV program with another class, and returned just as the children were leaving for lunch. All the booklets were stacked on the table, and I received permission to examine them in the empty room. There were 34 books in all. Three were empty; one had only pictures; 30 had pictures and a sentence. Of these 30, 24 fit one sentence pattern: "This is a Z." Another four consisted of that pattern with some embellishment: "This is a moon and a bird." "This is a house and here is the sun." "This is a tree with four apples." "This is a duck on the river." The twenty-ninth started with "these": "These are some Indians." The thirtieth was different in both form and content: "This little boy is dead." My first reaction was to wonder why the Bereiter-Engelmann program needs to spend time practicing "This is a Z." Later, I was struck by the greater structural variety of the sentences composed on their stands by the children using the Mackey-Thompson materials.

Before the midmorning break at the Lionel Road School (coffee for the teachers and recess for the children, though it's not called that in England), nine children sat down to work with the teacher at a large table. The teacher, Miss Wooldridge, had a large box of extra word cards which the children asked for; she listened as they read their completed sentences and, since I was present, asked each child if he would also read his sentences to the visitor; she wrote the sentences in their individual booklets and simultaneously monitored the activities of the rest of the group. Below are the first nine sentences. A slash line indicates that at the moment I saw the sentence in the stand, this was as far as it went; in other words, the slash line indicates some, though not necessarily all, of the stages in the composition of that sentence. The omission of periods and some capital letters is intended (Thompson, Schaub, and Mackay, 1968).

> "My mum take[s] me to school
> is my sister at school and   /   is my baby at home?
> Miss Wooldridge is a school because she looks like one (*sic*)
> I go to the picture[s] every Saturday morning
> I've   /   got a book all about Chitty Bang Bang at school
> I like David
> My cousin is skinny
> I brought Pip to school
> I like Sian"

Of the second set of nine sentences composed after the break, eight started with I + verb and the ninth was: "On Tuesday   /   the movie camera man is coming (this originally started with "the movie camera man" and then the entire sentence was shoved to the right to make room for "on Tuesday").

The simplest explanation of the differences between the Brize Norton and Lionel Road sentences is that when a picture is drawn first and a sentence then composed about the picture, the child is constrained toward the use of the "This is a Z" pattern. Without the picture there is no such constraint; any idea can be expressed, and more varied sentence patterns are needed. To the extent that this constraint does operate, it is imposed by the situation, not by this or any other teacher. What I observed may of course be un-representative, and it is undoubtedly true that the picture constraint doesn't operate for long. Many American observers have remarked on the high quality of children's writing (e.g., Featherstone, 1968), and most English children start writing in this way. But certainly the Mackay and Thompson materials cannot be considered *more* restrictive, as some critics have claimed.

As Mackay and Thompson watched children over many months, they discovered a developmental progression in the children's aware-ness of the structure of a spoken sentence. The following is a sum-mary of their findings (1968, pp. 112-15):

> Stage 1: The child simply lists words with no apparent link — "Dad" "boy" "girl" — and reads them as isolated words.
>
> Stage 2: The child composes on his stand a telegraphic sen-tence — "Children school" — but reads it as a complete sentence — "The children go to school."
>
> Stage 3: The child realizes that words are missing from the Stage 2 sentences and either adds them at the end — "Mum home my is at" — or selects the missing words after the telegraphic nouns and verbs and inserts them into their proper places.

Stage 2 seems to suggest that when children are five to six years old they may recapitulate, at the metalinguistic level of conscious aware-ness, the development from telegraphic to complete sentence which they went through at two to three years at the linguistic level of non-conscious oral speech. When materials such as these are used, the developmental progression is laid bare for the teacher to see. But as Mackay and Thompson point out, progress in this conceptual ability will not be revealed if the child only copies from a model which the teacher has written from the child's dictation, and it will be confounded with problems in handwriting and/or spelling unless he has whole words in some form to work with.

While watching children use the Mackay-Thompson materials, one realizes how much they must be learning about language. For example, in my short visit I noticed the following:

> Morphology: adding a separate card for *s* to verbs like *take* and

nouns like *picture*; composing *coming* by adding a card with *ing* to *come* so that the *e* is covered.

Syntax: inserting *on Tuesday* as a chunk at the beginning of a sentence.

Orthography: using a combination of small words and separate letters to compose longer words such as *h it s* as one boy in the six-year-old group did.

Professor Lovell at Leeds found in his research that mentally retarded children have an especially hard time understanding the derivation of compound nouns like *blackboard* on the Berko (1958) morphology test. The Mackay and Thompson materials have been strikingly successful with a small group of severely retarded children. Perhaps one reason is that they encourage the children to monitor their own language behavior, objectify it in words and/or letters on the stands, and then operate on it in various ways. This too is part of the metalinguistic level of our language ability (which Lovell considers part of Piaget's stage of concrete operations). Achievement of this level is not necessary for learning to talk; but it is probably necessary, or at least extremely helpful, in learning to read and write.

## The Gahagan-Bernstein Educational Program

Many people, in England as here, seem unaware that Basil Bernstein and his colleagues in the Sociological Research Unit of the University of London Institute of Education have designed and carried out a three-year educational program in infant and junior schools. A monograph on this work, especially for use by teachers, has been written by the two psychologists in the unit who were responsible for this part of the work (Gahagan and Gahagan, 1970). What follows gives a brief glimpse of what they did. All quotes, unless otherwise noted, are from the Gahagan's manuscript.

The educational program was designed to explore the implications of Bernstein's theory for education. As the Gahagans point out, "Bernstein's theory explicitly states that differences in usages of language do not arise out of *any deficiencies* in the speaker's tacit understanding of the linguistic system but arise out of the cultural constraints which affect the speaker's communicative intent. In Chomsky's sense the difference is at the level of *performance,* not competence" (emphasis in the original).

It was also designed to extend over three years — two in the infant school and one in the junior school; to require only 20 minutes per day and no more than £ 300 ($720) in materials for three classrooms over the three years; and to be feasible for ordinary teachers with no special qualifications, 40 children per class, and no aides. It was carried out in the East London borough of Newham, a working-class area with a disappointing record of educational attainments despite the outstanding effort of its Local Education Authority.

The 20-minute language training consisted of a variety of activities to improve three aspects of the children's verbal functioning:

(1) Attention and auditory discrimination. For example, a game like "Simon Says" or recognizing voices while wearing masks which shut out visual distractions.

(2) Explicit language use. An example would be a communication task in which two children sit on opposite sides of a screen. "Each child is given an identical set of materials which can be assembled. One child assembles his materials first. When he has completed his task, he has to *verbally* instruct his partner to produce an identical assembly. He is not allowed to show him. The other child can ask questions but must not look at his partner's assembly. When it is finished the two must compare to see whether the *instructions* have produced similar arrays." Or the teacher presents a dramatic situation and the children invent story and dialogue. Use of situations which deliberately involve role incongruity — "Children are skipping in a road and an old lady takes the rope and joins in" — prevents "the children using the ready-made clichés and phrases which they already associate with particular roles and which are, in any case, a formidable part of a restricted code."

(3) Language structure and vocabulary. Exercises include starting with a sentence like "Michael is going to the circus" and adapting it in time ("Last week . . .") or conditions ("If Michael had some money . . ."), and a game requiring the use of *and, and not, or,* etc., adapted from Bereiter-Engelmann.

During this 20-minute period, the class of 40 was divided into stable work groups of five children each, and the teacher circulated among them. Initially, each group was heterogeneous in overall language ability. Later, in each class one group of nontalkers was formed, for two reasons. "In the first case the children in them would become more salient for the teachers. . . . Secondly some of the children in these special groups would be forced to take up more assertive roles than they had been able to take up previously." In addition to this more formal language training, the Gahagans also helped the teachers to use ordinary situations throughout the school day for more explicit language use.

According to the research design, progress of the children in the three experimental schools ($E_1$) was to be compared with children in two sets of control schools: $C_1$, which were left entirely alone, and $C_2$, which received any Hawthorne effect on teacher motivation without a specific language component. Bernstein himself met with the three $C_2$ teachers for a seminar on many nonlanguage aspects of infant school teaching.

Problems of conducting research under the constraints operating here were great, and the Gahagans discuss them in simple and straightforward terms: uncontrolled variation among children and teachers, loss of sample children during the three-year period, and the selection and interpretation of appropriate measures. In the end, three different kinds of measures were used.

One was a set of nine tasks, designed especially for this research, which were related to the content of the language program but only indirectly related to regular classroom work. Of these nine, $E_1$ children were superior to $C_1$ and $C_2$ children "in their ability to generate sentences which in turn had an effect on performance in a simple learning task" (see more complete report in Gahagan and Gahagan, 1968); a small sample of $E_2$ children were better able "both to make and code finer discriminations among objects presented visually or tactually" (see Robinson and Creed, 1968, for more complete report on visual discrimination task); there were no significant overall effects of the language program in the other six tasks.

Results on four of these tasks are of interest. First, on all tasks but two, children initially high on the English Picture Vocabulary Test

(EPVT) were superior to children initially low. The two exceptions were creativity tests adapted from Wallach and Kogan (1965), thus replicating with younger children their finding "that verbal creativity is independent of verbal intelligence." Second, two tasks assessed the effects of training intended to sharpen "the children's perceptions of emotions and interpersonal relations and [extend] their vocabulary for this area of experience." The children were asked to describe stick figures, singly or in pairs. A High score was assigned to responses "which attributed emotion, motivation, volition or mood," while a Low score was assigned to "any atomistic or fragmentary response describing parts of the figure separately." Contrary to expectations, the $E_2$ children did not give more High responses. On the contrary, "A small number of $E_1$ children, mainly boys, seemed to have given precise, meticulous descriptions of the stick figures at the expense of wholistic, relational responses. For example, they specified the exact location of each arm and each leg in relation to the body, whether the heel was turned to the left or right, and whether a foot seemed to be raised off the ground." While this result was disappointing to the Gahagans, it fits exactly with findings in the United States on social class differences in coding styles (Heider, Cazden, and Brown, 1968). At least in this task, the Gahagan-Bernstein language program succeeded in making the children use language in more middle-class ways.

The second kind of evaluation, perhaps the most closely related to Bernstein's theory, depends on the children's answers to six questions on how mothers control children's behavior. "Before the children went to school for the first time a tape-recorded interview took place with the mothers. During this interview the mothers were asked six hypothetical questions about how would they control their child. Two and a half years later when the children were commencing their first term in the junior school the six questions in a slightly modified form were given to the children. . . . This provided us with a unique opportunity to examine whether the programme had in any way affected the children's perception of the control of others." Jenny Cook analyzed the answers into five control styles of which three were used in this evaluation. There were no differences between $E_1$ and $C_1$ children in frequency of "punishing" responses ("Mommy will whack him"), or "firmness" responses ("Mommy would tell him to be careful and watch what he was doing"), but the $E_1$ children offered significantly more of the "mediating" responses ("Mum will say, 'If you watch the program tonight, you can't see it tomorrow' "). "This style is linguistically more elaborated; it involves some manipulation of the authority relationship away from a coercive relation, and it indicates that the child has access to a range of alternatives in the context of control" (Gahagan and Gahagan, 1970: Appendix 2 by Brandis, Cook, and Goldberg). These results are all the more interesting when we note that the language of control was not a specific emphasis of the educational program.

The third and last kind of evaluation (Gahagan and Gahagan, 1970: Appendix 3 by W. Brandis), the most closely related to regular classroom work, used the English Progress Test (EPT), a written test of language use recently standardized on nearly 5,000 children. All project children in eight of the nine schools (excluding one $C_1$ school) were tested at the end of the third year. Whereas the proportion of the low EPT scores in C schools was higher than in the general population (27 out of 83), the proportion of low EPT scores in the $E_1$ schools was significantly lower (only 3 out of 50). This pattern does not reflect low WISC scores. In fact, the Hawthorne effect in the $C_2$ schools seems to have reduced the incidence of low WISC scores, while only the special language program in the $E_1$ schools reduced the incidence of low EPT scores. This effect held for the special subsample of 11 West Indian children, even though the language program was not specifically planned for their needs. In summary, Bernstein comments, "My impression overall was that the programme was especially helpful to children who potentially were candidates for low ability/attainment categories" (personal communication, 1969).

With such an imaginative program and such initially promising results even under difficult conditions, the Gahagan-Bernstein program provides an important base for further curriculum work. Because it also was designed to fit and supplement "prevailing infant school practice," it shows what can be done in a uniquely English way to enhance the development and use of language in school. I was all the more disappointed, therefore, to find that the compensatory education programs now starting in England were operating largely independently of this work and depending instead on less interesting curriculum ideas imported from the United States.

## Compensatory Education

In its recommendations for the improvement of primary schools for children up to age 11, the Plowden Report (1967, p. 441) gives first priority to the establishment of educational priority areas (EPA's). On the basis of such criteria as occupation of parents, size of families, and number of children who get free school meals or whose families receive "supplementary benefits" (welfare assistance in the United States), particular schools or groups of schools would qualify for preferential treatment (pp. 57-59). Such positive discrimination to close the "gap between the educational opportunities of the most and least fortunate children" (p. 65) should consist of the following steps:

Reduction of class size to 30.

Teacher aides for every two infant and junior classes.

Replacement or improvement of old and out-of-date buildings.

Provision of extra books and equipment.

Expansion of nursery education so that all children aged four to five who live in EPA areas should have the opportunity of part-time attendance and that perhaps 50 percent should have full-time places (p. 63).

The Plowden Report's discussion of the educational needs of deprived areas begins with a blunt statement that "what these deprived areas need most are perfectly normal, good primary schools alive with experience from which children of all kinds can benefit" (p. 51). The above measures are planned to redistribute educational resources to get such schools as fast as possible for the children who need them most.

Plowden also recommends that "research should be started to discover which of the developments in educational priority areas have the most constructive effects, so as to assist in planning the longer

term programme to follow" (p. 67). I cannot judge how much the
English government has begun to carry out the general recommendations for EPA areas, but I did learn about three research projects
which have been started by nongovernmental organizations. One of
these is the Nuffield Foundation Resources for Learning Project,
in which Mrs. E. Bay Tidy, a primary adviser, is trying to help
schools compensate for large classes and inadequately trained teachers by the use of educational TV and audio-visual aids. The other
two large-scale research programs are more directly related to the
language of young children: the Social Science Research Council
(SSRC) project directed by sociologist A. H. Halsey of the Department of Social and Administrative Studies at Oxford University,
and the Schools Council project in Compensatory Education directed
by Maurice Chazan and Phillip Williams of the Department of
Education, University College of Swansea, Wales.

The largest EPA research project is Halsey's. It is a three-year
project: six months for planning, two years for action research, and
six months for evaluation. It is based in five areas: The Deptford
area of London, Birmingham, Liverpool, the West Riding of Yorkshire, and Dundee, Scotland. The project staff in each area has considerable local autonomy, in true English style. However, one part
of the project will be nationally planned and evaluated — a preschool language program, directed by Allen Brimer, head of the
Research Unit of University of Bristol Institute of Education.

I met with members of Brimer's group when they were planning
the language program. Because they were faced in the spring of
1969 with planning for a program to begin that fall, consideration
was limited to curriculum ideas already available in a form which
could be given to teachers in five widely separated areas. Of such
materials, the group seemed inclined to the Peabody Language Development Kit. It would have to be adapted for English children:
items which don't exist in England, like corn on the cob, eliminated;
some labels substituted, like *biscuits* for *cookies*; and some grammatical forms substituted, like *have you got* for *do you have*. The
Kit consists of a set of language lessons, with all necessary materials
provided, more compatible with the philosophy of English nursery
school teachers than the Bereiter-Engelmann program which the

group rejected for that reason. All in all, it seemed like the kind of program which would give support to weak teachers without being too restrictive for more imaginative ones.

For the same reasons, the Peabody Language Development Kit is also being used in an experimental project conducted by H. L. Williams at the National Foundation for Educational Research (NFER, the organization most comparable to Educational Testing Service in the United States). Williams is working with five nursery schools in Slough, a town near Windsor Castle, which used to be a place on the London-Bath road where the horses were changed and is now partly an industrial park. Slough is proud of its tradition of nursery education and has been able to maintain a generous provision of nursery places, at least by comparison with many other local education authorities in England.

The head of one of the five nursery schools, Miss Hudson of the Cippenham School, agreed to try out the Peabody Kit and used it as the basis of daily 20-minute small-group language lessons during the 1968-69 school year. Miss Hudson feels that the children have benefited from the program, and initial test results support her impressions. But she is also changing the program as she goes along. Her children can go faster than the Kit manual recommends and she adds activities of her own design. Williams further plans to substitute some of the mathematics work from the infant schools (ideas from the Nuffield Mathematics Program, perhaps) for the arithmetic lessons included in the Kit.

One incident on the playground deserves a parenthetical note. As Miss Hudson was drawing the shapes, the children enjoyed calling out the names before she had finished. In the case of the triangle, they called out — correctly — when she had finished only one line, even though it could have been the beginning of a square or rectangle as well. That one line was diagonal to the seams in the playground cement, and diagonal to the school building wall. Evidently, in those children's concept of a triangle, diagonality was a more important marker than three-sidedness.

In Slough, another of the five nursery school directors, Mrs. Tait of Baylis Court Nursery School, was giving a selected group of 12 of her younger disadvantaged children a well-organized sequence of

language lessons based on concrete experiences such as shopping
expeditions and trips to the zoo. The NFER has been helping her
with clerical chores and evaluation.

In the Deptford part of the SSRC project under the direction of
Charles Betty, there may also be a second experimental preschool
language program for comparison with the Peabody Kit. It is being
designed by Mrs. Maureen Shields, a graduate student in linguistics
at University College, London, and a member of the teacher training
faculty at Goldsmith's College in Deptford. After I returned from
England, she wrote: "We are working on the principle that the
improvement of the language and intellectual skills of preschool
children should primarily be based on the improvement of the
teacher through a programme of support and inservice training designed to sensitise her to the importance and developmental features
of language. We hope thereby to enable her to exploit to the full
the linguistic and conceptual learning opportunities provided by the
child's own environment and activities both inside and outside the
nursery group" (personal communication, 1969). If it is actually
tried out and evaluated, Mrs. Shield's program should provide
important information on the effectiveness of language extension at
its best.[6]

The Schools Council project has three aims:

To provide screening techniques to enable children in need of
compensatory education to be identified at an early age.

To make longitudinal studies of infant school children in deprived
areas, with particular reference to their emotional development
and response to schooling.

To develop teaching programmes, involving materials in a variety

[6] By January 1970, Joan Heppenstall had assumed responsibility as the National Research Officer for Halsey's EPA project in charge of the nationally
coordinated part of the preschool work. Liverpool, Birmingham, and part of
West Riding were using the Peabody Kit; some schools in West Riding were
using an individual tutorial program based on Marion Blank's work (Blank and
Solomon, 1968). Dundee had developed its own language program consisting of
a sequence of concepts taught in structured small-group sessions and extended
during the rest of the school day. These four areas had agreed to a joint evaluation using the English Peabody Test and the Reynell Developmental Language
Scales (Reynell, 1969). The London part of Halsey's project was working separately with a language program for older children.

of media, which may be used to help culturally deprived children at the infant school stage (Schools Council, 1968, p. 5, or Schools Council, undated, p. 3).

The project will extend for three and a half years from the beginning in November 1967 and will be conducted in several areas in England and Wales. It is a project of longer duration than Halsey's, and more of the time will be used in defining further the dimensions of deprivation: which children (in an EPA area or out) and which aspects of their development need the most help. In spring 1969 work on program development was just beginning. Because all children go to infant schools at five years, whereas only a small percentage of children go to nursery schools (about 7 percent in 1965, according to the Plowden Report), the emphasis in all three parts of the project is on the infant school age range.

Neil Ferguson has been working on selecting, and in some cases designing, tests of intellectual and linguistic development. At the time of my visit, he was planning to use the following language tests:

A "structure of language" test based on Berko's (1958) "wug" test.

An auditory discrimination test, easier than the Wepman for five-year-olds, in which the children are asked to repeat pairs of words such as school-school or bud-but.

The English Picture Vocabulary Test, an adaptation of the Peabody Picture Vocabulary Test by Allen Brimer of Bristol and Lloyd Dunn of Peabody.

A short-term memory test of ability to repeat sentences.

Ferguson has also developed a symbols test which probably taps reading readiness but has language implications as well. First, the child is taught a set of visual symbols similar to pictographs used by some American Indian cultures. For instance:

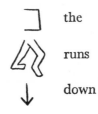

the

runs

down

Then the child is asked to "read" a string of such symbols:

⊐  ⚲  ⟨⟩  ↓     "The boy runs down."

One of the test questions turned out to be ambiguous but in a very interesting way. When asked "Where do these pictures say water runs?" some children say "Down hill" (the expected answer), and some children point to the symbols themselves. It is Ferguson's initial impression that the children who point to the symbols in response to *where* have lower overall scores.

In England as in the United States it is not always clear what compensatory education is supposed to be compensating for. The Plowden Report does not use the term as far as I can tell, but it does say that "the schools must supply a compensating environment" (p. 57). This suggests deprivations and "gaps" to be filled (Schools Council, undated, p. 9) in the *children*. But such a point of view seems at odds with other statements in Plowden that "what these deprived areas need most are perfectly normal, good primary schools . . ." (p. 51), which imply that the deficiencies are in schools, not in children.

The two members of the Plowden Commission whom I spoke to — Miss Grey in Wales and Miss Parry in Bristol — both seemed to take the latter view. But unlike some of their American colleagues in early childhood education, neither Miss Grey nor Miss Parry seem threatened by the special compensatory programs being developed by sociologists, educational psychologists, and other college professors. Miss Grey expressed the hope that these research projects would increase our understanding of all children. Miss Parry seemed to anticipate with some relish future competition between the best practices of the infant schools as she will document them and any program devised by the new research projects. She is confident that the best infant schools can match or surpass all competitors in benefits to children. Should it turn out that certain children need a special curriculum, she seems quite prepared to accept those results. If only reactions were as calm and minds as open to evidence in the United States.

## References

Barnes, D., et al. 1969. *Language, the learner and the school.* Baltimore, Md.: Penguin.

Berg, L. 1968. *Fish and chips for supper.* London: Macmillan.

Berg, L. 1968. *Risinghill: Death of a comprehensive school.* Baltimore, Md.: Penguin.

Berko, J. 1958. The child's learning of English morphology. *Word* 14:150-77. Also in S. Saporta, ed., *Psycholinguistics.* New York: Holt, Rinehart and Winston,1961, pp. 359-75.

Bernstein, B. In press. A critique of the concept "compensatory education." In C. B. Cazden, D. Hymes, and V. John, eds., *Functions of language in the classroom.* New York: Teachers College Press.

Bernstein, B. 1965. A socio-linguistic approach to social learning. In J. Gould, ed., *Penguin survey of the social sciences.* Baltimore, Md.: Penguin, pp. 144-68.

Bernstein, B., and Davies, B. 1969. Some sociological comments on Plowden. In R. Peters, ed., *Perspectives on Plowden.* London: Routledge and Kegan Paul, pp. 55-83.

Bernstein, B., and Henderson, D. 1969. Social class differences in the relevance of language to socialization. *Sociology* 3, no. 1: 1-20.

Bernstein, B., and Young, D. 1967. Social class differences in conceptions of the uses of toys. *Sociology* 1:131-40.

Blank, M., and Solomon, F. 1968. A tutorial language program to develop abstract thinking in socially disadvantaged preschool children. *Child Development* 39, no. 2: 379-89.

Cazden, C. B. 1970. Evaluating language learning in early childhood education. In B. S. Bloom, T. Hastings, and G. Madaus, eds., *Formative and summative evaluation of student learning.* New York: McGraw-Hill.

Cazden, C. B. 1968. Three sociolinguistic views of the language of lower-class children with special attention to the work of Basil Bernstein. *Developmental Medicine and Child Neurology* 10: 600-12.

Cazden, C. B. and Williams, S. 1969. *Infant school.* Newton, Mass.: Education Development Center.

Coleman, J., et al. 1966. *Equality of educational opportunity.* Washington, D.C.: U.S. Department of Health, Education, and Welfare, Office of Education.

Cremin, L. A. 1961. *The transformation of the school.* New York: Knopf.

Dixon, J. 1967. *Growth through English.* Reading, England: National Association for the Teaching of English. Also available: Champaign, Ill.: National Council of Teachers of English.

Featherstone, J. 1968. Experiments in learning. *The New Republic,* 14 December 1968, pp. 23-25.

Gahagan, D. M., and Gahagan, G. A. 1970. Talk reform: Explorations in language for infant-school children. *Primary socialization, language and education.* Vol. III. Sociological Research Unit Monograph Series, B. Bernstein, director. London: Routledge and Kegan Paul.

Gahagan, G. A., and Gahagan, D. M. 1968. Paired-associate learning as a partial validation of a language development program. *Child Development* 39: 1119-31.

Great Britain Central Advisory Council for Education. 1967. *Children and their primary schools.* (The Plowden Report.) Vol. 1. London: Her Majesty's Stationery Office.

Hawkins, P. R. 1969. Social class, the nominal group and reference. *Language and Speech* 12: 125-35.

Heider, E. R., Cazden, C. B., and Brown, R. 1968. Social class differences in the effectiveness and style of children's coding ability. In *Project Literacy Reports,* No. 9. Ithaca, N.Y.: Cornell University, pp. 1-10.

Jencks, C. 1969. A reappraisal of the most controversial educational document of our time — the Coleman Report. *The New York Times Magazine,* 10 August 1969.

Karnes, M. B. 1969. Research and development program on preschool disadvantaged children. Vol. 1. Washington, D.C.: U.S. Department of Health, Education, and Welfare, Office of Education.

Mackay, D., and Thompson, B. 1968. The initial teaching of reading and writing: Some notes toward a theory of literacy. Programme in linguistics and English teaching. Paper No. 3. London: University College and Longmans Green.

Macnamara, J. 1966. *Bilingualism in primary education.* Edinburgh: Edinburgh University Press.

Mitchell, C. I. 1969. Language behavior in a black urban community. Doctoral dissertation, Berkeley, Calif.: University of California.

Nuffield Foundation. 1967. *Beginnings.* New York: John Wiley.

O'Neil, W. A. 1969. Conference report: The Dartmouth Seminar. *Harvard Educational Review* 39: 359-65.

Plowden Report. See Great Britain Central Advisory Council for Education.

Reynell, J. 1969. *Reynell developmental language scales.* Slough, England: National Foundation for Educational Research.

Robinson, W. P., and Creed, C. D. 1968. Perceptual and verbal discriminations of "elaborated" and "restricted" code users. *Language and Speech* 11: 182-93.

Robinson, W. P., and Rackstraw, S. J. 1967. Variations in mothers' answers to children's questions, as a function of social class, verbal intelligence test scores and sex. *Sociology* 1: 259-76.

Schools Council. Undated. *Project in compensatory education.* Field Report No. 6. London: The Schools Council.

Schools Council Research Project in Compensatory Education. 1968. *Compensatory education: An introduction.* Swansea: University College of Swansea, Department of Education.

Schools Council Working Paper 29. 1970. *Teaching English to West Indian children: The research stage of the project.* London: Evans/Methuen Educational.

Squire, J. R., and Applebee, R. K. 1969. *Teaching English in the United Kingdom.* Champaign, Ill.: National Council of Teachers of English.

Thompson, B., Shaub, P., and Mackay, D. 1968. Manual to accompany the Schools Council literacy materials. London: Longmans Green. Not for sale.

Tough, J., and Oliver, B. 1969. *Language and environment: An interim report on a longitudinal study.* Leeds, England: University of Leeds Institute of Education. Mimeographed.

Wallach, M., and Kogan, N. 1965. *Modes of thinking in young children.* New York: Holt, Rinehart and Winston.

# PART III

## Evaluation

# 7

URSULA BELLUGI-KLIMA

## Some Language Comprehension Tests

Ability to use language adequately is considered to be essential to school success. If English sentences addressed to him do not convey the right meaning to the child, or if he cannot communicate his ideas plainly to others, the child is likely to have learning difficulties. To find out how the child is doing and to assess whether he is improving in his ability to communicate, teachers use a variety of measures. Some use standardized tests like the Peabody, which is a measure of vocabulary. However, how the child puts words together to form sentences is even more important than the size of his vocabulary. Specifically, it is important to know what children understand of the syntax of language, that is, not the meanings of individual words, but the particular patterns of words, regularities, and relationships of words in a sentence.

All adults know a great deal about the syntax of language as speakers of a language. We can demonstrate this by examining a sentence of Lewis Carroll's "Jabberwocky." Look at: "The slithy tove did gyre and gimble in the wabe." The main words in this sentence are all non-English words, combinations we've never heard before: "slithy," "tove," "gyre," "gimble," "wabe." The words we recognize are the small unstressed words of English which are not nouns or verbs — "the," "did," "in," "and." A string of words like "slithy," "tove," "gyre," "gimble," and "wabe" conveys nothing in the way of grammatical information. And yet, as we read the sentence, it seems to us that we can at least partially understand it. Let's examine what this partial understanding means and what the source of it is in the sentence.

Look first at "the slithy tove" and "the wabe." "Tove" and "wabe" seem to us to be nouns because they follow the definite article "the." "Slithy tove" seems to be a noun phrase like "dirty room," because the word between the article and the presumed noun ends in "y," which suggests an adjective. The "slith tove" would still seem to us a noun phrase, but perhaps more like "peanut butter." The "slithy tove" would seem like a noun phrase but like "the sailing ship," so we sense that "tove" is the head noun of a noun phrase and that "slithy" is an adjective modifying "tove." Now look at "did gyre and gimble." These words follow the noun phrase and seem to us to be the verb phrase of the sentence. We guess this because they follow the auxiliary verb "did" as in "he did do it." "Gyre" and "gimble" are connected by "and," which suggests that these are coordinate main verbs as in "run and play." Since they are not followed immediately by a noun phrase but instead by "in" plus a noun phrase ("the wabe"), we sense that they are intransitive verbs with a prepositional phrase following (as in "jump in the hay" and not like the verb in "I want some cookies," which requires an object). We notice that all this information is given to us by the relational words, the order of the words, and their relationship to one another, not by the words alone. If we rearrange the words in the same grammatical pattern, "The gimbly wabe did slithe and gyre in the tove," we notice that our sense of what is the subject, verb, adjective, etc., immediately changes.

We want to investigate, then, what children understand of the syntax of English. The common observation that children understand much more than they produce is made almost invariably without examining the limits of this understanding closely. In order to determine comprehension of syntax reliably, we need to set up carefully controlled situations in which the child gets minimal cues from the situation itself. We must make sure that the words are a part of the child's vocabulary, either by teaching him, or by using words known to most children of a certain age. We must construct test items so that the only way the child can give the correct answer is by comprehension of the particular construction we are interested in.

Take as an example the passive construction. To test, we must (a) Eliminate situational cues. Take the sentence "The apple was eaten by the doll." It is a well-formed passive sentence. We could ask the child to act it out for us and provide him with an apple and a doll. But even if he did perform correctly, it would not be conclusive evidence that he understood the passive construction. He might do exactly the same thing if we gave him the apple and the doll and said, "Do something with these." In his world, children are likely to eat apples, and not sit on them, put them on their heads, smash them, or be acted upon in any way by apples. This, then, is not a good test as it stands. (b) Make sure the child knows vocabulary so we are really testing understanding of syntactic constructions. Suppose we asked the child to act out "The construction was demolished by the superintendent." If he failed to perform correctly we would not know whether he failed to understand the words or the passive construction. In each case we must be sure that the objects are known to the child so we are testing understanding of syntax only. (c) Ensure that understanding of syntax is requisite for the correct answer. One way of solving this problem is to set up pairs of sentences which differ minimally with respect to the syntactic problem we want to study, and demand that correct responses require differentiating the two. With passive sentences, we might use sentences in which either the first or the second noun could be the subject or object of the verb. The verb "push" can take an animate subject and an animate object: a boy can push a girl and vice versa. This gives us the basis for a minimally contrasting pair of sentences, where the only difference between the two sentences is in word order, that is, in subject-object relations. "The boy is pushed by the girl," and "The girl is pushed by the boy." This seems a valid test for understanding of the passive construction in English.

A number of significant syntactic constructions can be tested for in this way. It seems a good method for examining comprehension since it requires the children to process the sentence in languagelike situations and to act out their understanding of the relationship of parts of a sentence.

## Comprehension Tests

Some comprehension tests for syntactic constructions will be suggested. In each case, these few examples can be extended to include other constructions, depending on what materials are available. Some basic materials for these tests include male and female dolls (with flexible limbs); a washcloth; doll's fork or spoon; blocks of assorted shapes and sizes; toy cat and dog or other animals; supply of marbles; clay; sticks of assorted colors, lengths, widths; balls; some doll's clothing; a bottle and cork; etc. Other materials which are ordinarily available in nursery school situations can be substituted if necessary, providing the problem still meets the demands set up in the previous section.

The objects for each problem should be set up on the table in such a way that they do not give cues to the solution of the problem (in terms of ordering or other cues) and in a way that the child has to make some change or movement to demonstrate comprehension of the problem. If the problem has more than one part, it need not necessarily be given in any fixed order. (Mixing up orders of presentation would minimize the effects of set.) The objects should be replaced in their original indeterminate position before asking another part of the problem.

The examiner should make sure at the onset of the problem that the child understands the words and actions involved. For example, for the problem "The boy is washed by the girl," the examiner would identify the boy doll and the girl doll and demonstrate how one washes the other, being careful not to give any cues to the problem. He might say, for example, "This is how we wash." He then checks the child's understanding of "boy," "girl," and "wash" before beginning. In the process it might be wise to change the order of presentation of boy and girl, so that no cues to ordering are given. Then the objects are set up in a standard way and the problem can be given.

The problems are set up in terms of levels of difficulty. This is based on order of appearance of constructs in children's speech in current developmental studies (Brown and others), on results of other comprehension tests (Brown, Fraser and Bellugi, 1964), and on proposed psycholinguistic research (Sinclair Olds, personal communication). Not all of these tests have been tried or standardized. They should be considered as proposals based on linguistic theory, psycholinguistic research, and developmental studies of children's speech.

## First Level Items

### Active Sentences

In the normal or most common English sentences, the first occurring noun is the subject or actor, and the noun which follows the verb is usually the object of the verb, or the recipient of the action of the verb. Thus, "John hits Mary" does not mean the same thing as "Mary hits John." A basic question, then, is does the child understand this subject — verb — object relationship? Given a verb, does he know that the noun which precedes the verb is generally the actor or subject and that the noun which follows the verb is the acted upon or object? We can test this by asking him to act out the following pairs of sentences (they need not be presented consecutively):

> The boy washes the girl.
> The girl washes the boy.
> The cat chases the dog.
> The dog chases the cat.
> The boy feeds the girl.
> The girl feeds the boy.

In each of the cases the objects are placed on the table in front of the child. Each is correctly identified and the action demonstrated, so that word meanings, referents, and conventions of demonstration are all known by the child, and we are really testing for subject–object relationships.

### Singular/Plural Noun

One of the early inflections to appear in children's speech is the inflection on the plural noun. However, it is a period of several months before these appear with any regularity where the situation and the context require them. In many sentences the plural inflection on the noun is redundant; that is, it may be signaled by some other means in the sentence. Notice the following examples: "There are two books." "These are spiders." "We have some plates." There are other cues to plurality in these sentences: the plural form of the copula "are," the plural of the demonstrative "these," and the form "some" with a count noun.

We want to test for comprehension of plural in the unusual case in which no other cues in the sentence indicate plurality. One method is as follows:

A small collection of objects (balls, marbles, clips, etc., as the problem requires) is placed on the table in front of the child. After they are identified, the instructions are given:

> Give me the marble.
> Give me the marbles.
> Give me the ball.
> Give me the balls.
> Give me the clips.
> Give me the clip.

### Possessive

A somewhat later inflection to appear in children's speech is the possessive inflection on nouns. Noun plus noun constructions appear earlier but without the inflection, as in "Mommy dress," "baby ball," etc. Here we want to examine the child's understanding of the possessive construction. In this case, there are two nouns occurring, and the first is a modification of the second. It is the second noun which is the head noun of the noun phrase: one could paraphrase "Mommy's shoe," as "the shoe which belongs to Mommy," or "the shoe which Mommy has." To test the child's comprehension of the possessive, we can set up some minimal pairs:

A small boy doll and a larger man doll. Identify one as the son and the other as the father.

> Show me the boy's daddy.
> Show me the daddy's boy.

A toy truck with a separate figure of a man driving the truck in the driver's seat.

> Show me the truck's driver.
>
> Show me the driver's truck.

A toy boat with the figure of a man on board who can be identified as the captain.

> Show me the captain's ship.
>
> Show me the ship's captain.

## Second Level Items

### Negative/Affirmative Statements

At a rather early stage, it is not clear that children process the negative aspect of a sentence when it is presented embedded in a sentence attached to the auxiliary verb. It is, in fact, often contracted with the auxiliary verb, generally unstressed, and not very salient. In some dialects, the difference between "I can do it" and "I can't do it" is only a minimal vowel sound change. We want to examine, then, if children process the negative (when attached to an auxiliary verb), and further, if they understand this as negating the sentence. This is not easy to demonstrate, but we might try the following pairs (note that each one uses a different negative and auxiliary combination):

Two dolls, one with movable arms; the other with arms that can't move. Demonstrate this without using the negative in sentences.

> Show me: The doll can't put his arms down.
>
> Show me: The doll can put his arms down.

Two dolls with flexible legs and a small chair or ledge. Show process of *sitting*.

> Show me: The doll is sitting.
>
> Show me: The doll is not sitting.

Two dolls and a hat which can fit on the head of either.

> Show me: The doll doesn't have a hat.
>
> Show me: The doll has a hat.

### Negative/Affirmative Questions

This problem is similar to the one above but involves *wh* questions rather than statements.

About six objects on the table, some of which are edible and some inedible; for example, a rubber ball, an apple, a cookie, a pencil, a flower, an orange. Examiner holds out hand:

What can't you eat?

What can you eat?

A girl doll and some objects of clothing plus other objects; for example, a blouse, some shoes, a piece of chalk, a candle, a coat, a fork. Examiner holds out hand:

What does she wear?

What doesn't she wear?

### Singular/Plural with Noun and Verb Inflections

We have mentioned that the noun ending for plurality is one of the early inflections to appear. Considerably later the verb ending for third person singular appears (present indicative tense). Notice the ending on the verb in the following contexts: "I go," "you go," "we go," "they go," but "he goes." For singular and plural sentences in the third person (or with other than pronominal subjects), we find that the inflection occurs on the verb for singular and on the noun subject for plural. Notice the following pair: "The bird sings," "The birds sing." At a period of overregularization, we sometimes hear children give the following singular plural forms: "The dog dig." "The dogs dig." We can test for understanding of singular/plural with noun and verb inflections as follows:

Two girl dolls lying down. Demonstrate *walking* for child (replace items after each part of problem).

Show me: The girl walks.

Show me: The girls walk.

Two boy dolls lying down. Demonstrate *jumping*.

Show me: The boys jump.

Show me: The boy jumps.

Two girl dolls and two washcloths (or brooms). Demonstrate *washing* (or *sweeping*).

Show me: The girls wash.

Show me: The girl washes.

### Modification (Adjectival)

As part of a noun phrase an adjective modifies or affects the meaning of the head noun of its noun phrase. Thus, we would guess that "slithy" modifies or affects the meaning of "tove" in the jabberwock sentence we considered. This applies only to the head noun of the noun phrase in which the adjective occurs. Thus, "big" in "The big boy ate an apple" applies only to the description of "boy" and is irrelevant to our understanding of "apple." We can test children's comprehension of adjectival modification by the following types of examples:

On the table are placed a large boy doll and a small boy doll and a large ball and a small ball. Identify only boys and balls for the child.

> Show me: The little boy has a big ball.
> Show me: The big boy has a little ball.

A round button, a square button, a round block, and a square block, are on the table.

> Put the round button on the square block.
> Put the square button on the round block.

A white dress with large black buttons. A black dress with large buttons (not black).

> Show me the dress with black buttons.
> Show me the black dress with buttons.

## Third Level Problems

### Negative Affix

Until now the negatives with which we are dealing have been sentence negations. There is another type of negation which has as its scope the word to which it is attached and not the sentence. We want to know if the child understands the effect of the prefix "un" before a word. Affixal negation is a late-appearing aspect of grammar in children's speech.

To test for understanding, we need to invent uncommon combinations of "un" and words. We want to guard against the possibility that children have learned both forms as separate vocabulary items as could be the case, for example, with "tied" and "untied."

In addition, we can test the effect of multiple negations with the negative affix. "John is happy" is clearly affirmative in meaning.

"John is unhappy" has as one semantic interpretation, "It is not the case that John is happy." "John is not unhappy" does not have the same interpretation as "John is happy," but the two negatives do in a sense cancel one another, and on a happiness continuum this sentence would certainly be more in the direction of "John is happy" than the previous one. We can easily add this dimension to our comprehension problems, then, in the following manner:

An array of blocks on the table. Some are flat on the table; some are piled on top of one another. As usual, replace in original position before asking another problem.

> Show me: The blocks are piled.
>
> Show me: The blocks are unpiled.
>
> Show me: The blocks are not unpiled.

Two jars or bottles with corks which fit in easily. One is corked and one uncorked. Let child try the process first.

> Show me: The bottles are corked.
>
> Show me: The bottles are not corked.
>
> Show me: The bottles are not uncorked.

A piece of cloth or dress with large snaps which are easily managed by children. Demonstrate and let children try snapping and unsnapping without using the words.

> Show me: The dress is not unsnapped.
>
> Show me: The dress is snapped.
>
> Show me: The dress is unsnapped.

### Reflexivization

Reflexives, like "John looked at *himself* in the mirror," also appear rather late in children's speech. Earlier forms might be the objective case pronoun instead of the reflexive pronoun ("I saw me"). We want to investigate the child's understanding that the *self* form of the pronoun after certain verbs refers back to the subject of the verb. We can test by the following means:

Two boy dolls on the table and a washcloth between them. Show action of washing. Introduce dolls by name, for example, "This is John and this is Bill."

> Show me: John washed him.
>
> Show me: John washed himself.

Two girl dolls with flexible arms. Show action of hitting but do not use reflexive. Introduce dolls by name, "This is Sally and this is Jane."

> Show me: Sally hit her.
> Show me: Sally hit herself.

Two girl dolls with flexible arms and doll spoon. Show action of feeding with spoon. Introduce dolls as above.

> Show me: Jane feeds her.
> Show me: Jane feeds herself.

## Comparatives

Comparatives are also rather late in appearance in the children's speech we have studied. We can investigate children's comprehension of comparatives in the following way:

A boy doll and a girl doll. Some piles of clay or marbles.

> Show me: The boy has more marbles than the girl.
> Show me: The boy has less clay than the girl.

Three red sticks of different lengths. Three blue sticks of different lengths. Identify red and blue.

> Give me: A red stick is shorter than a blue stick.
> Give me: A red stick is longer than a blue stick.

Three short sticks of varying thicknesses. Three long sticks of varying thicknesses. Identify short and long sticks.

> Give me: A short stick is wider than a long stick.
> Give me: A short stick is narrower than a long stick.

## Passives

Suppose we are presented with a sentence in which most of the words are familiar: "The boy lop washed zug the girl." We understand most but not all of the sentence. We could pick out "The boy" — "washed" — "the girl." "Lop" and "zug" are not words for us, and we do not know how they affect the rest of the sentence. If we were asked to act out this sentence without further information, we might make the best guess available to us and act out the aspects we understood. In English word order of noun phrase–verb, the noun phrase generally signals subject–verb–object, however we define these terms.

There is a set of sentences, however, which reverses the normal word order, namely, sentences in the passive voice. Thus "The car hits the train" becomes, in the passive voice, "The train is hit by the car." Notice that the two are equivalent in meaning, although the subject and object order are reversed. The full passive is another late-appearing construction in children's speech. It is often not understood or used until after four years of age. If younger children have only partial understanding of these sentences, we would expect something like our processing of "The boy lop washed zug the girl." When forced to make an interpretation, the younger children might act out the active form of the sentences, suggesting that they processed them as subject–verb–object like a normal English sentence with some unknown appurtenances added.

A boy doll and a girl doll on the table and a washcloth. Identify the boy and the girl and the action of *washing*.

>Show me: The boy is washed by the girl.
>Show me: The girl is washed by the boy.

A cat and a dog (stuffed toy animals). Identify each and show action of *chasing*.

>Show me: The cat is chased by the dog.
>Show me: The dog is chased by the cat.

A boy doll and a girl doll and a doll fork or spoon. Identify each and show action of *feeding*.

>Show me: The girl is fed by the boy.
>Show me: The boy is fed by the girl.

### Self-embedded Sentences

One of the most interesting properties of languages is that sentences can be indefinitely long; therefore, the set of possible sentences of a language is infinite. One way to achieve this length is by opening the sentence and adding constituents or sentences. Suppose the original sentence is "The boy chased the ball." We can insert "The boy lives on the next street," giving us: "The boy who lives on the next street chased the ball." Further we can insert "The boy lives in the white house at the top of the hill," giving us: "The boy who lives on the next street in the white house at the top of the hill chased the ball," and so on. The sentence could become indefinitely long by this process. We have embedded one sentence inside another.

We may want to know at what stage children learn to understand (or undo) self-embedded sentences. We can ask the child to act out sentences of these types as follows:

A boy doll and a girl doll in standing positions with flexible arms. Identify boy and girl and demonstrate *hitting* and *falling*.

> Show me: The boy that the girl hit fell down.
> Show me: The girl that the boy hit fell down.

A toy cat and dog. Identify and show *chasing* and *jumping*.

> Show me: The cat that the dog chased jumped.
> Show me: The dog that the cat chased jumped.

Relationships within self-embedded sentences are signaled by word order. In the sentences above, interpretation involves recognizing the outer sentence, "The boy fell down," and the inner sentence, "The girl hit the boy." An alternative ordering would change the sense of the inner sentence: "The boy hit the girl." These are difficult sentences, but we could test them as follows:

As above, a toy cat and dog, *chasing* and *jumping*.

> Show me: The cat that the dog chased jumped.
> Show me: The cat that chased the dog jumped.

# 8

DANIEL I. SLOBIN AND CHARLES A. WELSH

# Elicited Imitation as a Research Tool in Developmental Psycholinguistics[1]

Imitation probably is not an important device in language acquisition because the aspects of language which the child must acquire are not available to be imitated. He is exposed only to surface structures of sentences but what he must acquire are deep structures and the transformational rules which relate deep and surface structures. This argument has already been well developed by linguists and psycholinguists (e.g., papers in Smith and Miller, 1966), and we are not concerned in this paper with the role played by imitation in the natural situation of language acquisition. (This problem is discussed in Slobin, 1968.) Our present task is to determine what can be learned through the use of controlled, elicited imitations as a probe to discover the child's underlying linguistic competence. This is to say, we are concerned here with imitation as a device by which the investigator can learn about the child's language, and not as a device by which the child can learn about the adult's language.

The data examined here are part of a longitudinal study of linguistic development in one child. In keeping with the tradition of pseudonyms established by Brown and Bellugi's Adam, Eve, and Sarah (1964) and McNeill's Izanami (1966), we will refer to our

[1] This paper was written in April 1967 and was circulated in May 1968 as Working Paper No. 10 of the Language-Behavior Research Laboratory, Institute of International Studies, University of California, Berkeley.

Many of the ideas suggested here grew out of discussions with Mr. Barry A. Gordon, and many of the data were gathered and transcribed with the assistance of Miss Susan Carter. To both we extend our thanks.

subject as Echo. She is a precocious first child of graduate-student parents and has no siblings. This report is based on 1,000 elicited imitations, collected between the ages of 2:3:2 and 2:5:3. (Ages are given in years, months, and weeks.) By *elicited* imitations we refer to the child's repetition of a model sentence presented in a context calling for imitation, as opposed to the child's spontaneous imitation of adult utterances.[2] The time segment examined here is part of a continuing study of Echo's linguistic and cognitive development.

Psycholinguistic literature presents the following general picture of sentence imitation by two-year-olds (e.g., Brown and Fraser, 1963): the child repeats stressed content words in proper order with length and complexity of utterance not exceeding that of his spontaneous speech; that is, imitations have the same "telegraphic" character as the child's own utterances in which many function words and inflections are missing. Our intensive study of elicited imitations shows that all of these general statements are in need of modification. In addition, the "classical" picture gives no explanation of why imitation should be of this nature. One is simply left with the notion that the child scans a sentence and picks up some of the stressed, familiar words, working from left to right. We do not yet have a clear understanding of why he picks out the words he does nor of the extent to which his knowledge of the language determines the way in which he recognizes, stores, and reproduces sentences in immediate repetition. We are beginning to understand aspects of this process a bit more clearly and are in the process of building a model for sentence imitation — a model which will, we hope, also eventually reveal something about the way in which sentence recognition and comprehension takes place normally in both children and adults.

The general picture presented in the literature seems to hold true only if the model sentence is somewhat beyond the child's normal

[2] In the early stages of the investigation it was necessary to give the child explicit instructions to imitate (e.g., "Can you say . . ." or "Say . . ."). Such instruction soon became superfluous, as Echo apparently learned the subtle cues signaling a model sentence to be repeated. We are aware, however, of the problems posed by the fact that we have no way of assessing Echo's definition of the task or even if she always interprets the task in the same way.

sentence-processing span and is not anomalous. The following example corresponds well with this picture. (The model sentence, uttered by an adult, is given in capital letters; the child's imitation is given immediately below, in lowercase letters, followed by age in years, months, and weeks.)

1. THE PENCIL IS GREEN
pencil green (2:3:2)

Note that the child drops the article and copula as expected (though the article sometimes occurs in Echo's speech and imitations at this stage).

However, Echo also has much longer sentences in her free speech and at this same age can easily imitate another four-word sentence, such as:

2. TIGERS CAN DRINK MILK
tiger can drink milk (2:3:3)

And she can even successfully imitate much longer sentences (although often omitting article and copula), such as:

3. THE LITTLE BOY IS EATING SOME PINK ICE CREAM
little boy eating some pink ice cream (2:3:2)

Number of words, or number of morphemes, is clearly not a relevant measure of how much of a sentence a child can imitate. At this age, in her free speech, she has sentences as complex as, "It'll get burned in there," and sentences as long as, "This's Echo room, but then Daddy won't come in Echo room."

On the other hand, when she is somewhat older, and her grammar quite a bit more complex, she may drop out an entire embedded clause from a sentence which is not especially long in terms of morpheme count:

4. MOZART WHO CRIED CAME TO MY PARTY
Mozart came to my party (2:4:3)
(Mozart is a teddy bear.)

On the way toward discovering some of the determinants of Echo's imitations, we came across several interesting side phenomena which deserve passing mention.

If items are omitted from imitation, it may be that they are simply not heard. It has been frequently noted that the words omitted by the child are those most difficult for a transcriber to pick up from tape recordings of adult speech. Perhaps, then, one can simply get a child to imitate a normally omitted item by saying it especially loudly and clearly. And, in fact, one can sometimes get Echo to imitate an omitted element simply by stressing it, as in 5. (Underlining indicates stress; "..." indicates pause.)

>  5. THE PENCIL IS GREEN
>     pencil ... is green (2:3:2)

(Note that hesitation pauses are important cues to sentence processing.) Stress in the model sentence can also lead to alteration, as well as insertion of new material:

>  6. WE WERE HIDING
>     we was hiding (2:3:2)
>     WE WERE HIDING
>     we was hiding
>     WE WERE HIDING
>     we were hiding

It is interesting that properly positioned stress is maintained in the imitations presented in 5 and 6. However, one cannot simply state as a rule that any stressed item will be imitated and that position of stress will be maintained, because of examples such as:

>  7. THE BOY IS EATING AND CRYING
>     boy eating nuh crying (2:3:3)

Note, however, that stress is preserved in 7, although shifted to another position. The preservation of stress seems to be general, though its position is not always predictable. Even if all words are preserved, stress may still be shifted:

>  8. THERE ARE THE RED BEADS
>     there are the red beads (2:3:3)

The preservation of rhythmic and intonational aspects in imitation may be basic and perhaps universal. (For example, Fitzgerald [1966], in a study of spontaneous imitations by two-year-old speakers of Gã, a tone language, found errors in segmental phonology to occur far more frequently than distortion of the tonal and rhythmic structures of sentences imitated. In fact, 28 percent of segmental phonemes were incorrectly imitated, while only 2 percent of tonal phonemes were incorrectly imitated.)

We discovered, however, an important and intriguing exception to the generalization that rhythmic and intonational aspects of sentences tend to be retained in imitation. Echo consistently ignores repeated words in model sentences (9-11), unless the repeated word can be interpreted as an appropriate lexical item in the sentence (12).

> 9. MARK FELL FELL OFF THE HORSE
>    Mark fell off a horse (2:3:2)
>
> 10. I CAN CAN CAN EAT
>     I can eat (2:3:2)
>
> 11. I NEED NEED THE BALL
>     I need the ball (2:3:2)
>
> 12. I NEED THE BALL BALL
>     I need the ball ball (2:3:2)

This was true at 2:3:2 and also when repeated a month later, at 2:4:3. Echo ignored doubling or tripling of words, even if they were nonsense words.

> 13. KITTY WAS PERKING PERKING PERKING
>     THE ICE CREAM
>     kitty was perking the ice cream (2:4:3)

A moment's consideration convinces one of the adaptive necessity of such a strategy in sentence recognition. A child could simply not arrive at a reasonable grammar of a language if he tried to account for stutterings and false starts in the speech of his parents. To ignore successively repeated words in a sentence may be a basic instruction in the child's language acquisition device.

Examples 10 and 11 show that even if repeated words are all stressed, they are not picked up as repeated. Word repetition can, however, be recoded as stress in repetition:

> 14. WHERE WHERE IS KITTY?
>     where kitty? (2:3:2)
>
> 15. MOZART FELL OFF OFF THE TABLE
>     Mozart fell off the table (2:3:2)

It may be significant that the only function of word reiteration in English, namely, adverbial emphasis (e.g., "very, very good") can also be realized by stress (e.g., "<u>very</u> good"). These two devices seem to bear a certain equivalence both in the adult system and in Echo's imitations.

Before proceeding to more central findings, allow us to note briefly one more suggestive phenomenon which we have turned up in our investigations. Often Echo will spontaneously produce a fairly long and complex utterance. If this utterance is offered as a model immediately after its production, it will be (more or less) successfully imitated. However, if the very same utterance — i.e., the child's own utterance — is presented to the child ten minutes later, she will often fail to imitate it fully or correctly. For example:

16. IF YOU FINISH YOUR EGGS ALL UP, DADDY,
    YOU CAN HAVE YOUR COFFEE
    after you finish your eggs all up then you can have
    your coffee, daddy (2:5:1)

    *10 minutes later:*
    <u>you</u> can have coffee, daddy, after

    *half-hour later:*
    YOU CAN HAVE COFFEE, DADDY, AFTER
    YOU EAT YOUR EGGS ALL UP
    after you eat your eggs all up . . . eat your eggs all up

(The model sentences were offered by Echo's father. The sentence was still true on the second presentation.) It would seem that the child has an "intention to-say-so-and-so" — to use Willam James's phrase — and has encoded that intention into linguistic form. If that linguistic form is presented for imitation while the intention is still operative, it can be fairly successfully imitated. Once the intention is gone, however, the utterance must be processed in linguistic terms alone — without its original intentional and contextual support. In the absence of such support, the task can strain the child's abilities and reveal a more limited competence than may actually be present in spontaneous speech. Thus, whatever we discover in systematic probes of imitation must be taken as a *conservative* estimate of the child's linguistic competence.

These phenomena begin to point to a process which has occasionally been suggested in the literature; namely, that in repeating a sentence, one must filter it through one's own productive system. To use Piaget's terminology, a sentence, when recognized, is assimilated to an internal schema and, when reproduced, is constructed in terms of that schema. The question of interest, of course, is the extent to which such schemata correspond to the structures and principles of linguistic theory. We believe that our findings can begin to cast some light on that question.

Perhaps the most obvious examples of this sort of "assimilatory deformation," or "recoding in short-term memory," are cases in which one word is substituted for another, preserving meaning. This was the case in 6. Additional examples are:

17. TOMORROW THERE WILL NOT BE A LONG LINE
    won't be a long line (2:4:3)

18. THIS ONE IS THE GIANT, BUT THIS ONE IS LITTLE
    dis one little, annat one big (2:4:3)

This sort of rephrasing seems to be clear evidence that the child has retrieved the underlying meaning of the sentence and is encoding that meaning in a new form in imitation. This is a very basic point and one that reappears again and again in various forms.

Example 18 shows another very interesting finding in addition to the recodings of "giant" to "big" and "but" to "and." Note that the two propositions are inverted (with a change in conjunction). This is a very frequent finding in our data — and one that contradicts the generalization that order of elements is always preserved in imitation. If a sentence is a conjunction of two underlying propositions and the child understands both propositions, she will very frequently give the second proposition first in her imitation. We find many examples of this sort of inversion of sentences — conjoined by "and" — given a month earlier, as in 19 and 20, and more recently, as well, as in 21.

19. THE RED BEADS ARE HERE AND THE BROWN
    BEADS ARE HERE
    brown beads are over here; red beads over there (2:3:3)

20. THE RED BEADS AND BROWN BEADS ARE HERE
    brown beads here an' a red beads here (2:3:3)

### 21. MOMMY ATE THE CANDY AND MOMMY ATE THE ICE CREAM

mommy eat the ice cream and mommy eat a candy (2:5:3)

Note that Echo does not always give a literal repetition in these imitations but that she has clearly retained the two propositions. In 19 she even gives them as separate sentences, not conjoined by "and."

The inversion of conjoined sentences clearly indicates that Echo comprehends the use of "and" as a sentence conjunction. In fact, she will sometimes introduce it herself:

### 22. THE CANDY IS MARPLE. THE SHOE IS MARPLE.

... shoe marple an' a candy marple (2:3:3)

Not only does she comprehend the conjunction, but she must comprehend the structures of the two conjoined sentences as well. This is indicated both in 22 and elsewhere by inverted imitation of conjoined sentences with nonsense words occupying certain slots. Even though she has omitted the copula in her imitation, she must have correctly analyzed its function in order to have repeated the model sentences as she did. (A nonsense word in copular position will be imitated.)

Inversion of conjoined sentences also reveals something of Echo's strategy in sentence imitation. The data suggest that she has retained the general syntactic form of the model sentence — in this case, two sentences conjoined by "and" — and that what she is concerned with in output is to produce something of this general syntactic form. The exact content words and details of structure, however, are often lost, frequently resulting in the imposition of parallel construction, as in the imposition of "here" in the second part of 20.

This attempt to reproduce two parallel constructions can often take precedence over semantic content, as in:

### 23. THE BLUE SHOES AND BLUE PENCILS ARE HERE

blue pencil are here and a blue pencil are here (2:3:3)

It looks as if Echo has filled up so much of her short-term memory with information about the syntactic structure of the model sentences that she has no more room for all the lexical items. She clearly knows, however, what sorts of items are needed. And so, when she comes to the second noun phrase, she fills it appropriately with a noun from the model sentence — "pencil" — but in so doing uses the same noun twice. This matter of finding words to fit an abstract syntactic frame — or *lexical* instantiation of the structure — is a very common occurrence, even when parallel constructions are given in the model sentence. For example:

24. SUE ATE THE CANDY AND MOMMY ATE THE
    ICE CREAM
    mommy ate the ice cream and mommy eat the ice cream
    (2:5:3)

(Another example of this phenomenon appears in the second imitation of example 30, where "bread and jam" is imitated as "jam and jam.")

Note that imposition of parallel constructions on conjoined sentences can occur with or without inversion. The imitations in 20 and 21 are examples of the two phenomena combined: Echo repeats the second sentence and then imposes some aspect of its structure and/or content on the first. If the two sentences are quite simple, however, as in the "X is here" type, she can sometimes impose parallel constructions without inverting:

25. THE PENCIL AND SOME PAPER ARE HERE
    some pencil here and some paper here (2:3:3)

As a matter of fact, in the case of this simple sentence type, she can also perform the inverse operation of deleting and conjoining:

26. HERE IS A BROWN BRUSH AND HERE IS A COMB
    here's a brown brush an' a comb (2:3:3)

She can even do this occasionally with conjoined subject–verb–object sentences — in the following example even pronominalizing the subject noun phrase and deleting all redundant elements from the second sentence, retaining only the object:

27. DADDY IS GOING TO GET SOME COOKIES AND
    DADDY IS GOING TO GET SOME JUICE
    he gonna get some cookie and juice (2:3:3)

However, if the two conjoined sentences differ in structure, Echo has great difficulty in retaining both structures, indicating clearly that each syntactic structure takes up a certain amount of space in short-term memory. This is especially clearly revealed in hesitations, false starts, and imposition of parallel constructions, as in:

28. MOZART GOT BURNED AND THE BIG SHOE IS HERE
    Mozart got burned an-duh . . . big shoe got burned (2:3:3)

(Echo used the form "got burned" productively in spontaneous speech at this time.) Sometimes this difficulty leads to repetition of the same sentence twice:

29. THE BATMAN GOT BURNED AND THE BIG SHOE
    IS HERE
    big shoe is here and a big shoe is here (2:3:3)

Note that it is not predictable which of the two sentences Echo will start off with but that she retains the notion that there must be two sentences, even if she repeats the same sentence twice. (This should not be taken as an absolute statement, however. Occasionally, when distracted or tired or for other unknown reasons, Echo will repeat only one of two conjoined sentences. It is interesting that, in such cases, it is always the second of the two sentences which is repeated. This observation reflects the phenomenon noted above of frequent inversion in repetition of conjoined sentences.)

The imposition of parallel constructions suggests not only that syntactic structures are stored as abstract entities in short-term memory, but that the child may establish a set for a given syntactic structure, thus "blinding" her to other structures. This suggests an experiment such as that performed by Mehler and Carey (1967) in which subjects, after hearing ten sentences of the type "They are recurring mistakes," found it more difficult to hear an eleventh of the type "They are describing events." Although we have not yet performed such an experiment with Echo, we have one bit of suggestive evidence for a similar establishment of a set for a given syntactic structure:

30. THE BIRD ATE THE BREAD AND JAM
    bird ate a jam (2:5:1)
    THE BIRD ATE THE BREAD AND JAM
    bird ate the jam and jam
    THE BIRD ATE THE BREAD AND FLEW AWAY
    bird ate . . . ate ate ate

THE BIRD ATE THE JAM AND FLEW AWAY
bird ate the jam and flew away

The above examples give some hint of the rich data provided by imitations of conjoined sentences. About a month after we collected imitations of sentences such as those shown in 18 through 29 we noticed a very interesting phenomenon in Echo's imitations of conjoined sentences in which both sentences had the same noun phrase: she would pronominalize the second noun phrase, as in:

31. THE PUSSY EATS BREAD AND THE PUSSY
    RUNS FAST
    pussy eat bread and he run fast (2:4:3)

This suggests very strongly that she had mastered the transformation calling for pronominalization of repeated noun phrases in such structures and that she was using this transformation in producing an utterance based on the underlying structure she had retrieved from the model sentence. She would even introduce a pronoun for a second noun phrase if it were deleted in the model sentence:

32. THE OWL EATS CANDY AND RUNS FAST
    owl eat candy . . . owl eat the candy and . . . he run fast
    (2:4:3)

Her hesitations and false starts indicate she was working hard to produce an imitation matching her image of the model. The introduction of a pronoun for the second noun phrase suggests that her rules do not yet allow for the total deletion of a repeated noun phrase in this sort of structure, although note that she was able to do so a month earlier in the simple structure represented in example 27.

At this age (2:4:3) she imitated sentences with embedded *who*-constructions in similar fashion, suggesting a comprehension which exceeded her productive competence. For example:

33. MOZART WHO CRIED CAME TO MY PARTY
    Mozart cried and he came to my party (2:4:3)

The parallel interpretation of conjoined sentences and of sentences with embedded *who*-constructions is especially clear in the following two examples, in which Echo's imitations of two different structures are virtually identical:

34. THE OWL EATS CANDY AND THE OWL RUNS FAST
   owl eat candy and he run fast (2:4:3)

35. THE OWL WHO EATS CANDY RUNS FAST
   owl eat a candy and he run fast (2:4:3)

These examples suggest that "who" is ignored. It could be that Echo scans her memory of the model sentence looking for subject–verb–object (SVO) constructions; and, if a subject occurs twice, or if a second subject is lacking, she will use "he" in that position. In addition her rules require that she join the two SVO constructions with "and."

Further support for such an imitation device comes from numerous examples such as the following:

36. THE MAN WHO I SAW YESTERDAY GOT WET
   I saw the man and he got wet (2:4:3)

Note that word order in the first part of the sentence is not maintained. In her free speech, Echo uses "I" only in the subject position and so appropriately uses "I" as the subject of sentences such as these. Thus, it is not clear from such examples whether *who*-constructions of this sort are understood in adult fashion or whether a more simple rule of seeking SVO sequences is being applied. In sentences such as 33 and 35, "who" could simply have been ignored and SVO could still have been appropriately retrieved. Unfortunately, our data are scanty in this regard, but we have some suggestive evidence that this *who*-construction is beginning to be understood and that it enters as a more compact way of pushing together in surface structure information which might be represented by two propositions — two "S's" — in deep structure. The clearest example is the following intriguing substitution in successive imitations of the same model sentence:

37. THE MAN WHO I SAW YESTERDAY RUNS FAST
   I saw the man who run fast
   I saw the man and he run fast (2:4:3)

The notion that Echo may have been looking for SVO relations in the model sentences intrigued us and so we constructed sentences in which it would be very difficult to retrieve the underlying structure if the necessary transformation rules were lacking. These were sentences in which the rate of information transmission in surface structure was very compact, due to various deletions, and in which embedded sentences were not introduced by cue words such as "who" or "that." For example, two sentences can be simply conjoined by "and": "The book hit the boy and the boy was crying." The first sentence can be embedded in the second in various ways, e.g., "The boy who the book hit was crying." In addition, "who" can be deleted, giving: "The boy the book hit was crying." When Echo was 2:5:1 and 2:5:2, we administered systematically varied sets of sentences of these types. These structures were clearly beyond her competence and were generally treated as word lists. For example:

> 38. THE BOY THE BOOK HIT WAS CRYING
>     boy the book was crying (2:5:1)

Order was not necessarily preserved in these imitations. For example:

> 39. THE HOUSE THE BOY HIT WAS BIG
>     boyhouse was big (2:5:1)

Occasionally reorderings looked as if Echo were searching for words with which to instantiate an SVO relation. For example:

> 40. THE BOY THE CHAIR HIT WAS DIRTY
>     boy hit the chair was dirty (2:5:2)

Such extractions of SVO relations seemed to occur only when they were semantically plausible in Echo's speech. She would never say "boy hit house" or "boy hit marble" — perhaps because "hit," for her, means "to strike with the palm of the hand." She would, however, extract "boy hit chair" and "boy hit man" from such sentences. It seems that Echo's words bear both syntactic and semantic markers and that she will form SVO constructions when she can identify not only two nouns and a verb, but a constellation of nouns and a verb which can form a semantically acceptable relationship.

Echo frequently extracted SVO relations, in similar fashion, from scrambled sentences. For example:

> 41. THE MAN THE BOY THE BOOK HIT TORE WHO
>     boytheman tore the book who (2:5:2)

There is, however, an important relation between sentence development and memory span which should not be overlooked here.

Echo will perfectly imitate ungrammatical or anomalous sentences if they are short enough for her to hold an auditory image in short-term memory. For example, as young as $2:3:2$, she repeated all possible order of the three words "John loves company." The same, of course, is true of adult repetitions of deviant sentences. One must only call on mechanisms of assimilatory deformation when the material — because of its length or complexity or both — exceeds short-term memory capacity.

When sentences are short and simple enough, Echo makes amusing attempts to assimilate new words into her existing grammatical schemata, thus showing a fine sense of the role of context in providing clues for the lexical categorization of unknown items. One of the most amusing examples is her imitation of the following sentence, offered after one of the authors had read what he considered a singularly poor paper on transformational grammar and child language:

42. CHOMSKY AND VERITAS ARE CRYING
    Cynthia and Tasha . . . cry $(2:5:3)$

Cynthia and Tasha are friends of Echo. Clearly she has realized that the sentence calls for two proper nouns, and she has substituted two more familiar names which bear more phonological information than is available in short-term memory. This is especially evident in apparent search for unfamiliar words, as in:

43. EX POST FACTO I SEE THE QUARTER
    eptah . . . quarter I see ekso . . . ekso, ekso,
    ekso, ekso $(2:5:3)$

Examples 42 and 43 do not agree with the finding of Smith, Shipley, and Gleitman that children "tend not to listen to adult speech beginning with unfamiliar words" (Smith, 1966, p. 3). Not only did Echo attend to unfamiliar words appearing in sentence-initial position, but she frequently repeated them without difficulty, as in:

44. CUI BONO IS THE QUARTER
    cui bona a quarter $(2:5:3)$

This is a very sketchy summary of what one can discover from carefully examining about 1,000 elicited imitations in one child over a period of less than three months. We hope to have demonstrated that the method is a fruitful one. It must be used, we believe, together with running collections and analysis of spontaneous speech. This very preliminary analysis has convinced us that sentence recognition and imitation are filtered through the individual's productive linguistic system. More specifically, we believe that we can tentatively offer the following generalizations:

Echo can spontaneously utter sentences which she cannot imitate. On the other hand, she can give *recoded* imitations of model sentences which exceed her productive capacities.

Emphasis can lead her to repeat words she would normally omit from imitation, but she generally ignores repeated words in imitating model sentences.

If she comprehends a sentence, she need not repeat it in the order given. Reordering can also take place as a result of imposing SVO constructions upon model sentences.

The process of sentence recognition includes retrieval of both form and content. Syntactic structures take up space in memory, and frequently content will be sacrificed to the retention of form in immediate, rote imitation. On the other hand, if content has been retrieved and stored, it may be encoded in the child's own syntax in imitation.

A fine-grained analysis of repeated imitations of systematically varied model sentences can reveal aspects of the child's theory of syntax, including transformational rules and the syntactic and semantic markers borne by lexical items.

## References

Brown, R., and Bellugi, U. 1964. Three processes in the child's acquisition of syntax. *Harvard Educational Review* 34:133-51.
Brown, R., and Fraser, C. 1963. The acquisition of syntax. In C. N. Cofer and B. S. Musgrave, eds., *Verbal behavior and learning*. New York: McGraw-Hill, pp. 158-97.
Brown, R., Fraser, C., and Bellugi, U. 1964. Explorations in grammar evaluation. In U. Bellugi and R. Brown, eds., *The acquisition of language*. Monographs of the Society for Research in Child Development 29, no. 1. Chicago: University of Chicago Press.

Fitzgerald, L. K. 1966. Child language: An analysis of imitations by Gã children. Unpublished paper, University of California, Berkeley.

McNeill, D. 1966. The creation of language by children. In J. Lyons and R. J. Wales, eds., *Psycholinguistics papers*. Edinburgh: Edinburgh University Press, pp. 99-115.

Mehler, J., and Carey, P. 1967. The role of surface and base structure in the perception of sentences. *Journal of Verbal Learning and Verbal Behavior* 6: 335-38.

Slobin, D. I. 1968. Imitation and grammatical development in children. In N. S. Endler, L. R. Boulter, and H. Osser, eds., *Contemporary issues in developmental psychology*. New York: Holt, Rinehart and Winston, pp. 437-43.

Smith, Carlota S. 1966. Two studies of the syntactic knowledge of young children. Paper presented at Linguistics Colloquium, Massachusetts Institute of Technology.

Smith, F., and Miller, F. A., eds. 1966. *The genesis of language: A psycholinguistic approach*. Cambridge, Mass.: Massachusetts Institute of Technology Press.